Tax Processes for Businesses

(Finance Act 2023)

Tutorial

for assessments from 29 January 2024

Jo Osborne

Published by Osborne Books Limited
Tel 01905 748071
Email books@osbornebooks.co.uk
Website www.osbornebooks.co.uk

Design by Laura Ingham

Printed by CPI Group (UK) Limited, Croydon, CR0 4YY, on environmentally friendly, acid-free paper from managed forests.

British Library Cataloguing in Publication Data
A catalogue record for this book is available from the British Library

ISBN 978-1-911681-03-8

Contents

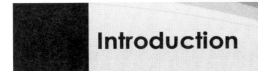

Introduction

Qualifications covered

This book has been written specifically to cover the Unit 'Tax Processes for Businesses' which is a mandatory Unit for the following qualifications:

AAT Level 3 Diploma in Accounting

AAT Level 3 Certificate in Bookkeeping

AAT Diploma in Accounting – SCQF Level 7

The book contains a clear text with worked examples and case studies, chapter summaries and key terms to help with revision. Each chapter concludes with a wide range of activities, many in the style of AAT computer-based assessments.

Osborne Study and Revision Materials

Additional materials, tailored to the needs of students studying this unit and revising for the assessment, include:

- **Workbooks:** paperback books with practice activities and exams
- **Student Zone:** access to Osborne Books online resources
- **Osborne Books App:** Osborne Books ebooks for mobiles and tablets

Visit www.osbornebooks.co.uk for details of study and revision resources and access to online material.

1 Introduction to Value Added Tax

this chapter covers...

This chapter is an introduction to Value Added Tax (VAT) and the way in which businesses are affected by it.

It contains:

- a **definition** of Value Added Tax as a tax on sales and consumer expenditure
- the distinction between Value Added Tax as an **input tax** (on goods and services a business buys) and an **output tax** (on goods and services a business sells)
- an **overview** of the way in which a business is affected by VAT, including the processes of:
  - entering transactions involving VAT into the accounting system of a business
  - extracting data from the accounts to work out the amount of VAT a business may have to pay, or reclaim
  - completing the VAT Return
- details of the various **VAT rates**
- details of where to find **information** about VAT
- an explanation of the process by which a business becomes **VAT-registered** with HMRC (the government body that regulates and collects VAT) describing:
  - who has to register
  - when they have to register and when they can deregister
- an explanation of how businesses are affected by the workings of **HMRC**, including inspections of the VAT records of a business

WHAT IS VALUE ADDED TAX?

a definition

Value Added Tax (VAT) is a tax on the sale of goods and services.

This means that VAT is:

- a tax on **consumer expenditure** – it is charged on most goods and services and affects everyone in the UK, whether they are a business or an individual

- an **indirect tax** – as the tax is collected by the seller at the time of sale, consumers do not normally notice they are paying it, unlike Income Tax which is a direct tax clearly shown on a payslip

VAT is not only charged in the UK; many countries charge VAT (or a similar sales tax), and at varying rates.

VAT is an important source of revenue for the government; the higher the rate of VAT, the more the government receives to finance its spending needs.

HM Revenue & Customs and VAT law

The government body that regulates and collects VAT in the UK is **HM Revenue & Customs**, which also regulates other areas of taxation such as Income Tax and excise duties. The common abbreviation for this body is **HMRC**, which we will use in this book.

VAT law in the UK is mainly governed by the Value Added Tax Act (1994), which is then amended by annual Finance Acts, and other regulations issued by the government. Further regulation is provided by the **VAT Guide** (Notice 700) issued by HMRC. This Guide, together with supplementary notices, explains and interprets the VAT regulations. These are all available on the HMRC website – www.gov.uk/government/organisations/hm-revenue-customs.

AN OVERVIEW OF VALUE ADDED TAX

Before explaining VAT in detail, we will first explain the whole process of a business – a **supplier** of goods or services – that charges VAT and eventually pays the amount due to HMRC.

This process starts with registration.

registration for VAT

Businesses that supply goods and services will normally charge VAT, unless there is no VAT payable, for example, as is the case for the sale of food or young children's clothes. By law, businesses must **register** with HMRC for charging VAT if their annual taxable turnover reaches a certain level.

There is a registration threshold set by the government each year, normally in the Budget. The VAT threshold is currently £85,000, which has remained unchanged since April 2017.

If, at the end of any month, a business's total taxable turnover (sales) for the previous twelve months exceeds the current registration threshold or is likely to exceed this figure during the next 30 days, that supplier must, by law, register with HMRC to become what is known as a **taxable person**.

If at any point the value of taxable turnover in the next 30-day period alone is expected to be more than the registration threshold, the supplier must register without delay (see page 10 for more details of the registration regulations).

The effect of this registration means that the supplier (taxable person):

- must charge VAT on taxable supplies (ie goods and services)

  – this is known as **output tax**

- can reclaim VAT paid on most business supplies received

  – this is known as **input tax**

Most businesses are run to make a profit, so more money will be received from sales than is spent on supplies. This means that most businesses will charge more VAT (output tax) than they pay (input tax). The difference between these two amounts is calculated and submitted online in the **VAT Return** (see page 7). This difference must then be paid to HMRC.

VAT – a tax on the end user

At this stage it is important to note that VAT is a tax which is ultimately paid by the **final consumer** of the goods or services.

If a member of the public buys a computer for £720 and the VAT rate is 20%, the amount paid includes VAT of £120 (ie 20% of £600). The buyer of the computer bears the cost of the VAT, but the VAT is actually paid to HMRC by all the businesses involved in the manufacturing and selling process.

This is illustrated by the diagram on the next page. The right-hand column shows the amount of VAT paid to HMRC at each stage in the process. The supplier of raw materials, the manufacturer and the shop all pay to HMRC the difference between VAT collected on sales (outputs) and VAT paid on purchases (inputs), but this amount is collected from the next person in the process. It is the **consumer** at the end of the chain of transactions who pays the VAT bill. This VAT is paid to the retailer, but as you can see from the diagram, the VAT is actually paid at various stages to HMRC.

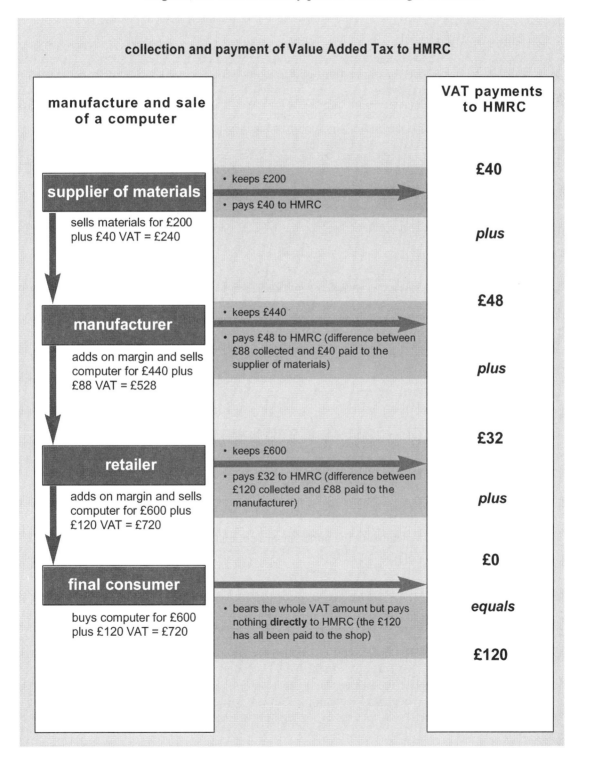

collection and payment of Value Added Tax to HMRC

manufacture and sale of a computer

VAT payments to HMRC

supplier of materials
- keeps £200
- pays £40 to HMRC

sells materials for £200 plus £40 VAT = £240

£40

plus

manufacturer
- keeps £440
- pays £48 to HMRC (difference between £88 collected and £40 paid to the supplier of materials)

adds on margin and sells computer for £440 plus £88 VAT = £528

£48

plus

retailer
- keeps £600
- pays £32 to HMRC (difference between £120 collected and £88 paid to the manufacturer)

adds on margin and sells computer for £600 plus £120 VAT = £720

£32

plus

final consumer
- bears the whole VAT amount but pays nothing **directly** to HMRC (the £120 has all been paid to the shop)

buys computer for £600 plus £120 VAT = £720

£0

equals

£120

the flow of VAT data – financial transactions

Later in this book we will look in detail at how VAT data from the accounting system of a business is used to provide the figures to be entered on the VAT Return.

This chapter provides an overview of how the process works, starting with financial transactions and finishing with the preparation of the VAT Return and payment being made to HMRC.

Study the diagram below and read the text that follows.

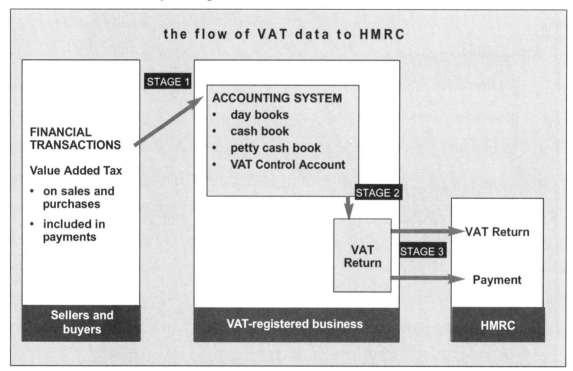

Stage 1 – financial transactions to accounts

The first stage is the transfer of VAT information from the documents that are generated by financial transactions into the accounting system of the business.

The process is as follows:

■ VAT figures on invoices and credit notes, and any VAT included in payments are calculated and transferred to the day books, cash book and petty cash book in the accounting system of the business.

■ The VAT totals from these accounting records are then transferred to a **VAT account** in the ledger accounts; this account forms a collection point for these totals and other VAT figures which are transferred from the accounts. Accounting software will carry out this process automatically.

Stage 2 – accounts to VAT Return

■ Figures from the **VAT control account** and other accounts that record sales (outputs) and purchases (inputs) are then transferred to the VAT Return (see below).

■ Acquisitions of goods made in Northern Ireland from EU Member States are also included, together with the VAT totals which relate to these. The VAT Return works out the total amount owing to (or owed by) HMRC by deducting input VAT from output VAT.

Stage 3 – VAT Return to HMRC

■ The final stage is the submission of the VAT Return by the due date (usually every three months) to HMRC. This form is completed online and submitted electronically to HMRC.

■ Payment of VAT due to HMRC must also be made electronically by the appropriate due date.

VAT Return
01 Jan 24 to 31 Mar 24

VAT due on sales and other outputs	1	£469.26
VAT due on intra-community acquisitions of goods made in Northern Ireland from EU Member States	2	£0.00
Total VAT due (the sum of boxes 1 and 2)	3	£469.26
VAT reclaimed on purchases and other inputs (including acquisitions from the EU)	4	£200.00
Net VAT to be paid to Customs by you (the difference between boxes 3 and 4)	5	£269.26
Total value of sales and all other outputs excluding any VAT	6	£4,266
Total value of purchases and all other inputs excluding any VAT	7	£1,000
Total value of intra-community dispatches of goods and related costs, excluding any VAT, from Northern Ireland to EU Member States	8	£0
Total value of intra-community acquisitions of goods and related costs, excluding any VAT, made in Northern Ireland from EU Member States	9	£0

Example of an online VAT Return generated by accounting software

RATES OF VAT

There are currently three rates of VAT in the UK:

- standard rate   20%
- reduced rate (eg on domestic energy and children's car seats) 5%
- zero rate (eg on most food)   0%

There are also goods and services on which no VAT is charged, eg membership subscriptions, insurance, and charitable donations. These are **exempt** supplies. There are also some goods and services that are outside the scope of VAT so VAT cannot be charged or reclaimed on them. Examples of out of scope items are statutory fees, like the London congestion charge, and donations to a charity for which nothing is received in return.

Zero-rated supplies are not the same as exempt supplies, although the result is the same, ie no VAT is charged. This is explained below.

zero-rated supplies

Zero-rated supplies are goods and services that are taxed at 0%. This means that the supplies are taxable, but the government has decided that no VAT should be charged. This is normally because the goods are an essential part of household spending and to tax them would be unfair on the less well-off as there is no choice whether to buy them. Or it may be because the item is essential to safely carry out a task. Examples of zero-rated supplies are:

- most food bought in shops, but not in restaurants
- young children's clothes and shoes
- transport – eg bus and train fares
- newspapers, magazines, and printed books
- motorcycle helmets

An important point here is that businesses selling zero-rated goods are allowed to reclaim the VAT charged (input tax) on supplies that they have bought. For example, there was no VAT charged on this book, but the publisher was able to reclaim the VAT paid on the costs of the publishing process and the sales and marketing costs.

The situation with exempt supplies is quite different.

exempt supplies

We have seen that zero-rated supplies are chargeable – at 0% VAT. However, VAT is not chargeable at all on exempt supplies. A business that only supplies VAT-exempt goods or services cannot reclaim any input VAT on purchases.

Examples of supplies that are generally exempt include:

- health and dental care
- education and training
- betting and gambling
- burials and cremations

For further information on zero-rated and exempt supplies you should refer to the 'VAT Guide' which illustrates these points further. This is available at www.gov.uk/guidance/vat-guide-notice-700.

SOURCES OF VAT INFORMATION

The administration of VAT is a complex process, and organisations (and students) need regular, easy access to accurate information and advice.

Some of this information changes frequently, which brings with it additional challenges. VAT rates may vary, and each government Budget brings in further changes and new measures. On the previous page we saw the percentage VAT rates which were correct when this book went to press, but VAT rates may change, so it's a good idea to check that they are still current.

VAT information online

Online information about VAT is readily available on the internet. The most useful site is:

- **www.gov.uk**

    This is the website for all government departments, and many government agencies and public bodies. One organisation included on this site is HMRC which has a direct link to a VAT section on its home page. The principal document produced by HMRC is the VAT Guide (Notice 700). This is a huge document which has many links to supplementary documents and notices, but it is reasonably well indexed and has search boxes which means you can usually find what you are looking for.

There is also regular updating information – which includes explanations of changes in VAT – published on the websites of the major accounting firms after each Budget.

VAT information – paper-based sources

The problem with paper-based resources is the danger that they may be out-of-date by the time you read them, so always check the publication date carefully. Useful sources of reference material include:

- the HMRC VAT Guide in paper format

- online reference material subscribed to by accounting firms

- tax updates published by firms of accountants on their websites

But remember to check the publication date!

VAT information – other sources

Another way that you can keep up-to-date with changes in VAT practices is to attend relevant Continuing Professional Development (CPD) updates. These will be organised and run by the professional accounting bodies that have specialist staff with detailed up-to-date knowledge on VAT matters. In addition to this, obtaining relevant CPD by meeting with other accounting professionals and reading relevant articles in journals and magazines will help to ensure you have the most current VAT knowledge available.

REGISTRATION FOR VAT

VAT registration – the regulations

In certain circumstances, a business selling goods and services on which VAT is chargeable must apply to HMRC to become VAT-registered. **Compulsory registration** is required:

- when, at the end of any month, **taxable supplies** over the previous 12 months has exceeded the VAT registration threshold set annually by the government (£85,000 in Finance Act 2023) – the business must notify HMRC within 30 days of the end of the month when the threshold was exceeded. Registration is then effective from the first day of the second month after the threshold is exceeded. For example, if a business exceeds the threshold in May 2023, it must notify HMRC of this by 30 June 2023. Registration is then effective from 1 July 2023. This is the **historic turnover test**

- when annual taxable turnover is expected to exceed the VAT registration threshold (£85,000 in Finance Act 2023) during the next 30 days, the business must register before the end of the 30-day period. Registration is then effective from the start of the 30-day period. For example, in October 2023, a business secures a large sale for £90,000 which will be paid for on 26 October 2023. The business must notify HMRC by 30 October 2023, and registration will be effective from 1 October 2023. This is the **future turnover test**

- if the value of taxable turnover in the next 30-day period alone is expected to exceed the registration threshold (£85,000 in Finance Act 2021)

If a business does not register on time it may be fined as it will not be collecting tax due to HMRC. Registration for VAT is normally completed online.

Businesses that supply zero-rated goods and services are included in these regulations, although they may apply for exemption from registration.

It is unlikely that a business will do this as it would mean that it would be unable to reclaim any VAT on goods and services it has purchased.

failure to register

It is critical that a business registers for VAT if the supplies that it makes are chargeable, and it exceeds the registration threshold. A business that fails to register when it is required to do so may face a civil penalty for **failure to notify**. This is calculated as a percentage of the **potential lost revenue** (PLR), which depends on:

- whether the failure to register was deliberate or not
- whether the business was prompted by HMRC to register
- how long it is since the VAT was due

The table below shows the percentages that are applied. It is worth noting that penalties will not be applied if there is a reasonable excuse for a business not having registered.

penalties for failure to register for VAT as a % of Potential Lost Revenue (PLR)

type of behaviour	within 12 months of tax being due		12 months or more after tax was due	
	unprompted	prompted	unprompted	prompted
non-deliberate	0-30%	10-30%	10-30%	20-30%
deliberate	20-70%	35-70%	20-70%	35-70%
deliberate and concealed	30-100%	50-100%	30-100%	50-100%

Importantly, if HMRC discovers that a business has not registered for VAT when it should have done, it will treat the business as though it had registered on time and will expect VAT to be accounted for as if it had been charged. The VAT which should have been charged is potential lost revenue for HMRC. In these circumstances the business has two choices in respect of this VAT, which it has not included in its invoices. It may either:

- allow HMRC to treat the invoices as VAT inclusive and absorb the VAT which should have been charged, or
- account for VAT as an addition to the charges already invoiced (ie add VAT on to the original total on the invoice) and attempt to recover this VAT from its customers.

In practice the second option is difficult to administer, and customers are not obliged to pay the VAT. Consequently, there have been cases of profitable businesses that have not registered and have been 'discovered' by HMRC after a period of years: these businesses have had to pay all the VAT they should have charged from their own funds and have been bankrupted as a result.

who should register for VAT?

In the eyes of HMRC, an individual or organisation that is in business is known as a **taxable person** and should register for VAT if sales are over the registration threshold. Taxable person includes:

- sole proprietors (ie individuals)
- partnerships (ie groups of individuals)
- limited companies or groups of companies
- clubs and associations
- charities
- any other organisation or group of people acting together under a particular name, for example an educational establishment

taking over a going concern

If you intend to take over a business that is already a going concern, it may already be registered for VAT. However, you may need to register at the date you buy the business. The VAT rules for the purchase of a business as a going concern are complex. Basically, if the total of your turnover and the turnover of the business you are taking over exceeds the VAT registration threshold then you must be registered for VAT from the day that the business is transferred to you.

exception from registration if threshold is temporarily exceeded

The taxable turnover of a business may exceed the VAT threshold temporarily, for example due to a significant one-off sale. In this circumstance the business must write to HMRC with evidence as to why it believes its VAT taxable turnover will not go over the deregistration threshold (£83,000 in Finance Act 2023) in the next 12 months.

Note: if turnover goes over the VAT limit temporarily and the business does not notify HMRC within 30 days, it will not be able to request an exception. Instead it will have to register and then apply to be de-registered.

a business or not a business?

Only a **business** can register for VAT and become a 'taxable person'.

A 'taxable person' is in business when they:

- earn an income by carrying out a trade, vocation, or profession
- provide membership benefits as a club or association in return for a subscription

■ carry out activities as a charity or other non-profit making body

In order to qualify as being a business these activities must be carried out regularly and over a period of time. This would exclude hobbies and other private activities, even if they involve buying and selling. If you occasionally sell your belongings on a website such as eBay or Vinted, for example, or sold at the occasional car-boot sale, that would not be considered to be a business activity. However, if you did this on a regular and frequent basis to make money, you would be classed as a business and would need to become VAT-registered, if your VAT taxable turnover reached the VAT threshold.

non-registered businesses

Businesses that have a turnover below the annual registration threshold do not have to register for VAT or charge VAT, which can be useful for a business owner that sells to an individual. The business will be more competitive than a VAT-registered business as it does not have to charge VAT to the consumer for goods and services. This means that many small traders such as plumbers, electricians and gardeners who sell their skills may be able to benefit by not having to register for VAT. However, if the trader is not registered, they cannot reclaim VAT paid on supplies that they have bought.

It is worth noting that this is not the same as a dishonest VAT-registered business who says to their customers, 'If you pay me cash in hand you won't have to pay the VAT'. In this case this is an illegal attempt to defraud HMRC (and ultimately the taxpayer!) of VAT due.

voluntary registration

A supplier with VAT taxable turnover below the annual registration threshold may **voluntarily register** for VAT, even if they are not required to do so. This is normally done because the business will benefit from claiming back input tax on purchases, eg if the business sells zero-rated goods, such as books or children's clothes. VAT collected on sales will be £zero, but VAT will have been paid by the business on many of its expenses. Being registered for VAT effectively reduces the cost of the purchases, as money equal to the amount of VAT paid will be refunded to the supplier.

Another advantage of voluntary registration is that it may be possible to reclaim VAT on purchases of goods and capital assets held on the effective date of registration for VAT. There is normally a time limit of four years for goods, and six months for services.

Remember, the main point of voluntary registration is for a business to take advantage when the goods or services it supplies are **zero-rated**.

If a business that supplies standard or reduced-rated supplies decides to register for VAT voluntarily, this will increase the cost to any customers who are not VAT-registered.

A business that supplies only **VAT-exempt** goods or services cannot register for VAT, and so will not be able to reclaim any input VAT on its purchases.

Voluntary registration carries with it all the responsibilities of VAT registration: a business must keep all the required VAT records and submit a VAT Return on the due dates. If a business is receiving regular refunds of VAT, it can improve its cashflow by choosing to submit VAT returns monthly rather than quarterly.

practicalities of registration

■ registration can be carried out online through https://www.gov.uk/register-for-vat or by downloading and completing the necessary forms

■ when a business has been registered for VAT, a registration certificate will be issued giving full details of registration, including the **VAT number** which must be quoted on VAT invoices issued by the business

■ VAT paid by the business on expenses incurred setting up the business may normally be reclaimed

■ a business must charge VAT at the appropriate rate on its sales as soon as it has registered for VAT

changes to VAT registration

If any of the following details about a VAT-registered business change, the business must notify HMRC within the time limit detailed in the table below.

notification of changes to VAT registration

name, trading name or address	Within 30 days
partnership members	Within 30 days
agent's details	Within 30 days
bank account details	14 days in advance
change in business activity	Within 30 days

voluntary deregistration

If a business finds that its annual taxable turnover falls – or is likely to fall – below the deregistration threshold (£83,000 in Finance Act 2023), the business can choose to **voluntarily deregister** for VAT, if it feels it is beneficial to do so. For example, this might be when a sole trader is running down the business before retirement, or if they decide to work part-time. In order to deregister, the business must provide evidence that its taxable supplies will not exceed the deregistration limit in the next 12 months.

Deregistration can be done online or by completing a paper based VAT7 form and will be effective from the date HMRC receives the request to deregister, or an agreed later date.

compulsory deregistration

A business that is making taxable supplies may be required to deregister for VAT. The main reason for compulsory deregistration would be because the business stops making taxable supplies.

A business must notify HMRC within 30 days of it ceasing to make taxable supplies. Deregistration is effective from the date of cessation.

Other circumstances that also mean a business must deregister are:

- the business is sold – although the new owner of the business may apply to keep the same VAT registration number

- the legal status of the business changes – this may be from sole trader to partnership or limited company. The new business may apply to keep the same VAT registration number

- a VAT group the business is a member of is disbanded or the business joins a VAT group

- the business joins the Agricultural Flat Rate Scheme

REGULATION BY HMRC

We have seen in the last few pages that HMRC is the official body with which businesses must register for VAT purposes, and that HMRC acts as regulator and enforcer for all matters connected with VAT. This is in addition to its responsibilities for other types of taxation and for excise duties. The requirements of HMRC are therefore legal requirements.

This affects businesses in a number of different areas, including:

- registration (already covered earlier in the chapter)

- submission of VAT Returns and other documentation

- keeping VAT records

- inspecting the records of registered businesses

We will deal with the last three of these in turn.

VAT Returns to HMRC

As we will see in Chapter 4, the **VAT Return**, which sets out the calculations of the VAT that will need to be paid to (or reclaimed from) HMRC, is the main online form that VAT-registered businesses must complete. It must be accurate, and it must be submitted on time.

business records to be kept

HMRC requires that all VAT-registered businesses should maintain a full set of accurate business records. These should provide evidence that the VAT charged and claimed on the VAT Return is correct.

The records that should be maintained include:

- annual accounts, including the statement of profit or loss

- VAT accounts and any associated working papers

- ledger accounts, cash book, petty cash book, sales and purchases day books

- sales invoices (copies) and purchase invoices

- credit or debit notes issued or received

- bank statements and paying-in slips

- import and export documentation

- records of daily taking (if appropriate) such as till rolls

- orders and delivery notes

- any related correspondence and contracts

- a valid VAT certificate of registration

retention period for business records

HMRC requires that businesses keep their financial records for at least six years. HMRC regularly sends VAT inspectors to businesses to check through these records and ensure that:

- the records are accurate and complete

- the business is complying with all the VAT regulations

- the business is paying (or claiming for) the correct amount of VAT

Failure to keep the necessary business records will result in a penalty of £500.

storage of VAT records

Although some businesses will keep paper copies of VAT records for the required six years, businesses are permitted to store VAT records **electronically**. With the requirements of Making Tax Digital (covered in more detail in Chapter 4), most businesses will keep their accounting records, and consequently their VAT records, digitally.

control visits and inspections

There is often a picture given of a visit from VAT officers being a nerve-racking and unwelcome experience. This will only be the case if the business has something to hide and has been avoiding payment of VAT that is due. The frequency of a VAT visit will depend on how large or complex the business is, or on how reliable the business has proved to be in the past. HMRC will normally give a business seven days' notice of a visit and will confirm what information the VAT officers will want to see, how long the visit is likely to take, and if they want to inspect the business's premises. If necessary, the business can ask for the visit to be delayed.

HMRC can also visit without an appointment and may also telephone a business about its VAT.

VAT officers check businesses to make sure that their VAT records are up-to-date. They also check that amounts paid to (or claimed from) the government through HMRC have been correctly calculated.

They will examine the VAT records and ask questions of the business owner, or the person responsible for the VAT records. A visit may take as little as a few hours or may last several days – depending on the nature of the business.

When the inspection has been completed, the VAT officer will review with the business the work carried out during the visit and explain any areas of concern that they have identified, discuss them with the business owner (or manager) and agree any future action needed. If any adjustment needs to be made to the amount of VAT payable, this will also be discussed, and the amount of over or underpayment confirmed.

VAT inspections are not necessarily bad news: the inspectors will sometimes give advice and suggest ways of improving the accuracy and efficiency of the accounting function of the business. However, if there is a major fraud taking place, they will soon identify the problem and take action to recover the underpaid VAT, and enforce any penalties that are due.

Chapter Summary

- Value Added Tax (VAT) is a tax on sales of goods and services, making it a tax on consumer expenditure.

- VAT is administered and regulated by HMRC, a government body with responsibility for a wide range of taxes.

- VAT is paid by the final consumer, but is collected and paid to HMRC by the businesses involved in the selling and manufacturing processes.

- A VAT-registered person must pay the VAT charged on sales (output tax) less tax on purchases (input tax) to HMRC. If input tax exceeds output tax a refund is due. The payment or refund is calculated on the online VAT Return.

- VAT is charged at different rates: standard rate of 20% (most supplies), reduced rate of 5% (eg on domestic fuel) and zero rate (eg on food). With the exception of zero rate, the Government may change the rates of VAT from time to time. VAT is not charged on goods and services that are exempt from VAT.

- The most up-to-date and comprehensive source of information about VAT can be found online on the government website: www.gov.uk/browse/tax/vat.

- A business must register for VAT if its annual taxable sales exceed (or are likely to exceed within 30 days) the £85,000 VAT registration threshold.

- The 'taxable person' must be in business and can be an individual, partnership, limited company, club, association or charity which charges for its goods or services.

- A business with annual sales below the VAT registration threshold may voluntarily register if it believes there is an advantage in doing so, for example if it sells zero-rated goods (no VAT charged) and is able to claim back input VAT paid on expenses related to those sales.

- If the annual VAT taxable sales of a VAT-registered business fall below the deregistration threshold of £83,000, that business can apply to deregister for VAT.

- A business must submit an accurate online VAT Return by the due date to HMRC.

- As part of its regulatory role, HMRC will regularly inspect VAT-registered businesses, partly to ensure that they are paying the correct amount of VAT and also to provide help and advice where it is needed.

Key Terms

Value Added Tax (VAT)	a tax imposed on the sale of goods and services
indirect tax	a tax which is imposed indirectly on consumers by taxing their spending
HMRC	the government body that regulates and administers the collection of taxes – including VAT
VAT Guide 700	the online guide published by HMRC which explains the workings of VAT
taxable person	a business that is registered for VAT – the taxable person can be a sole trader, a partnership, a limited company, a group of companies, a club or association, or a charity
output tax	VAT on sales of goods and services
input tax	VAT on purchases of goods and services
VAT Return	the HMRC VAT form that calculates VAT to be paid or refunded by deducting input tax from output tax
standard rate	the percentage rate at which VAT is charged on most goods and services, currently 20%
reduced rate	a reduced rate allowed for socially beneficial items such as domestic fuel, currently 5%
zero-rated supplies	supplies which are liable to VAT, but at 0% VAT rate
exempt supplies	supplies that are not liable to VAT at all
VAT registration	the formal procedure by which a business registers with HMRC and will then charge VAT and account for VAT due to HMRC
VAT threshold	an amount set by HMRC for annual taxable sales of a business, above which the business must register for VAT (£85,000 in Finance Act 2023)
voluntary registration	VAT registration of a business with annual turnover below the VAT threshold
deregistration	where the annual sales of a VAT-registered business fall below a certain threshold (£83,000 in Finance Act 2023) and the business applies to HMRC to cease to be VAT-registered and no longer charge VAT
VAT visits and inspections	control visits to VAT-registered businesses by HMRC VAT officers who check that VAT is being charged and accounted for correctly

Activities

1.1 VAT charged by a supplier on a sales invoice is known as:

(a)	Input tax	
(b)	Output tax	
(c)	Consumer tax	
(d)	Supplier tax	

Which **one** of these options is correct?

1.2 The form summarising total input tax and output tax which a business must regularly submit to HMRC is known as:

(a)	A VAT Return	
(b)	A Sales List	
(c)	A Registration Return	
(d)	A VAT Control Account	

Which **one** of these options is correct?

1.3 The amount of VAT due to HMRC can be calculated as follows:

(a)	Output tax plus input tax	
(b)	Output tax minus input tax	
(c)	Output tax divided by input tax	
(d)	Output tax multiplied by the VAT rate	

Which **one** of these options is correct?

1.4   A purchase invoice with VAT for taxable supplies is being processed by the VAT-registered business that receives it. What will be the effect of this invoice on the amount of VAT due to be paid to HMRC by that business?

(a)	It will decrease the amount due to be paid	
(b)	It will increase the amount due to be paid	
(c)	It will have no effect at all	
(d)	It depends on the annual taxable sales threshold set for VAT registration	

Which **one** of these options is correct?

1.5   A VAT-registered business receives a credit note from a supplier. The document shows a VAT amount of £6.70. What effect will this have on the amount of VAT due to HMRC from this business?

(a)	It will increase by £6.70 multiplied by the VAT rate	
(b)	It will decrease by £6.70, which is the VAT amount on the credit note	
(c)	It will stay the same because the input VAT will cancel out the output VAT	
(d)	It will increase by £6.70, which is the VAT amount on the credit note	

Which **one** of these options is correct?

1.6   A customer buys goods costing £180 from a shop with £30 VAT included in this amount. This will eventually be paid over to HMRC by which of the following?

(a)	The customer	
(b)	The customer and the shop	
(c)	The manufacturer and the supplier of the materials for the product	
(d)	The manufacturer and the supplier of the materials for the product and the shop	

Which **one** of these options is correct?

1.7   A zero rate of VAT appearing on an invoice for goods supplied means which of the following:

(a)	The supplier is not registered for VAT	
(b)	The goods are VAT-exempt	
(c)	The goods are chargeable for VAT, but the rate of VAT is 0%	
(d)	The purchaser does not have to pay the VAT amount that is shown	

Which **one** of these options is correct?

1.8   According to HMRC regulations, Marina must register for VAT if:

(a)	The value of her taxable supplies over the last six months has exceeded the VAT registration threshold set by HMRC	
(b)	The value of her taxable supplies over the last twelve months has exceeded the VAT registration threshold set by HMRC	
(c)	The estimated value of her taxable supplies over the next 12 months is likely to exceed the VAT registration threshold set by HMRC	
(d)	The estimated value of her taxable supplies over the next six months is likely to exceed the VAT registration threshold set by HMRC	

Which **one** of these options is correct?

1.9   Which of the following is entitled to register for VAT?

(a)	An individual who sets up a shop in the town where she lives	
(b)	An individual who occasionally sells his possessions on an online auction site	
(c)	An individual who advertises in the local paper the contents of a house he has inherited	
(d)	An individual who is an amateur pilot and sometimes charges people for rides in her plane	

Which **one** of these options is correct?

1.10   Which of the following might be a reason for a trader to voluntarily register for VAT?

(a)	The total of his taxable supplies over the last twelve months has exceeded the registration threshold	
(b)	He would be able to deregister in the future, even if his annual sales exceeded the annual threshold	
(c)	His business would benefit because it would be able to reclaim input VAT on VAT-exempt invoices	
(d)	His business would benefit because it would be able to reclaim input VAT on standard-rated invoices	

Which **one** of these options is correct?

1.11   HMRC states that VAT records should be kept by a business for a minimum of how long?

(a)	Six months	
(b)	Six years	
(c)	Twelve months	
(d)	Twelve years	

Which **one** of these options is correct?

1.12   HMRC regularly sends its VAT officers to visit all businesses that:

(a)	Have applied for VAT registration	
(b)	Have applied for voluntary registration	
(c)	Are already VAT-registered and have an annual sales turnover of £1 million or more	
(d)	Are already VAT-registered, to ensure they are complying with the VAT regulations	

Which **one** of these options is correct?

1.13 Aleisha starts trading on 1 January 2023. Her taxable sales to the end of June 2023 are £70,000. July turns into a bumper month and by the end of July her total taxable sales for the year so far are £90,000. By what date does Aleisha need to register for VAT?

(a)	31 July 2023	
(b)	30 August 2023	
(c)	31 December 2023	
(d)	1 January 2024	

Which **one** of these options is correct?

1.14 Boris is the owner of a building in Knightsbridge which he has just had converted into a hotel. He plans to start trading on 1 February 2023. Taxable sales in February 2023 are expected to be £120,000. By what date should Boris register for VAT?

Enter the correct date below.

2 VAT and business documents

this chapter covers...

This chapter will look at how VAT works in practice. It explains how VAT should be shown on a variety of business documents and also how a number of common VAT calculations are carried out.

The documents covered include:

- *standard VAT invoices used in the UK, simplified VAT invoices and modified invoices*

- *invoices for zero-rated and VAT-exempt supplies of goods and services*

- *pro-forma invoices*

- *VAT receipts*

- *e-invoicing*

- *reverse charge invoicing*

VAT calculations need to be carried out from time to time in business. In this chapter, we look at a number of calculations, including those for:

- *VAT amounts using a variety of rates*

- *VAT which is included in the total amount on a document but not shown as a separate amount*

- *VAT when discounts are offered*

You will also need to know about tax points for VAT. A 'tax point' is the point at which a supply of goods or services is treated as taking place for VAT purposes. This chapter explains how 'basic' and 'actual' tax points are worked out, and then how the tax point is determined for advanced payment, deposits, good or services that are supplied on a continuous basis, and goods that are supplied on a sales or return basis.

VAT INVOICES

full VAT invoices

A VAT-registered business that sells goods or services must give or send a VAT invoice to the purchaser within 30 days of the earlier of the date of supply or receipt of payment. This invoice contains information about the goods or services supplied. An electronic or paper copy of the invoice must be kept on file by the business.

In order to claim back the VAT paid on a purchase, a VAT-registered customer must receive a valid VAT invoice from the supplier. The contents of a VAT invoice required by HMRC are set out in the **VAT Guide**.

A full VAT invoice (see examples on the next two pages) must show:

- a unique, sequential invoice number
- the invoice date
- the time of supply (the tax point) if different from the invoice date
- the supplier's name and address and VAT registration number
- the customer's name and address
- a description of the goods or services sufficient to identify the goods or services

  for each description:
  - quantity of goods (eg items) or the extent of the services (eg hours)
  - rate of VAT charged per item (clearly stating if it is exempt or zero-rated)
  - amount payable excluding VAT
  - the rate of any discount per item
- the total net amount payable, excluding VAT
- the rate of any cash discount offered
- the total amount of VAT
- the unit price or rate (eg for a service), excluding VAT

You will know from seeing different types of invoices that there are many varying formats used, and other details included, eg trade discounts, codes for products, customer accounts and terms and conditions, not to mention the total amount due including VAT! However, HMRC states in the VAT Guide 700 that the items listed above **must** be present on the invoice. Any other details and features may be added to the document to fit in with the requirements of the supplier.

Have a look at the invoices on the next two pages which illustrate these requirements.

SALES INVOICE

Trend Designs

Unit 40 Elgar Estate, Broadfield, BR7 4ER
Tel 01908 765365 Fax 01908 7659507 Email lisa@trend.u-net.com
VAT Reg GB 0745 4172 20

invoice to

Crispins Fashion Store 34 The Arcade Broadfield BR1 4GH		

invoice no	787906
account	3993
your reference	1956
date/tax point	21 04 20-4

deliver to

as above

details	quantity	unit price	amount (excl VAT)	VAT rate %	VAT amount £
Schwarz 'T' shirts (black)	20	5.50	110.00	20	22.00
Snugtight leggings (black)	15	12.50	187.50	20	37.50

terms
Net monthly
Carriage paid

Total (excl VAT)	297.50
VAT	59.50
TOTAL	357.00

This invoice has been issued by Trend Designs, to Crispins Fashion Store on 21 April (the tax point). All the requirements of a VAT full invoice are met – both items sold are charged at the standard rate of tax and the unit price is shown.

The VAT total of £59.50 will be recorded as output tax for Trend Designs and input tax for Crispins Fashion Store. There is no discount offered, and the buyer has to settle the full £357 a month after the invoice date.

──── SALES INVOICE ────

Paragon Printers

Partners: Edwin Parry, George Dragon
Unit 43 Elgar Estate, Broadfield, BR7 4ER
Tel 01908 765312 Fax 01908 7659551 Email Ed@paragon.u-net.com VAT Reg GB 0745 4672 71

invoice to

Prime Publicity Ltd 4 Friar Street Broadfield BR1 3RG	

invoice no	787923
account	3993
your reference	47609
date/tax point	07 05 20-4

deliver to

as above

details	unit price	amount (excl VAT)	VAT rate %	VAT amount £
Printing 2000 A4 leaflets	189.00	189.00	zero	00.00
Supplying 2000 C4 envelopes	75.00	75.00	20	15.00

terms
Net monthly
Carriage paid

Total (excl VAT)	264.00
VAT	15.00
TOTAL	279.00

This invoice has been issued by Paragon Printers, to Prime Publicity Limited on 7 May (the tax point) for goods delivered. In this case there are two rates of VAT involved: printing is zero-rated, and stationery is standard-rated. Where there is more than one VAT rate, the rates and VAT amounts must be quoted. The VAT total of £15.00 will be recorded as output tax for Paragon Printers and as input tax for Prime Publicity Ltd. There is no discount offered, and the buyer has to settle the full £279.00 a month after the invoice date.

time limits for issuing a VAT invoice

A VAT invoice must be issued within 30 days of the earlier of:

■ the date of supply

■ receipt of payment

The invoice, which can be paper or electronic (see below), is deemed to have been issued when it is either handed, or sent, to the customer.

electronic invoices

Electronic invoicing is increasingly used by businesses as invoices can be automatically generated by accounting software. Advantages of e-invoicing include:

■ instant transfer of the invoice to the customer

■ rapid access and retrieval

■ reduced storage and postage costs

■ possible improved cash flow as the customer receives the invoices more quickly and so is likely to pay more quickly

■ more secure transfer

■ easier to access in dispute handling

The electronic format used must be secure and may be a structured format such as XML or an unstructured format such as PDF.

Electronic invoices must contain the same information as paper invoices.

invoices for zero-rated and exempt supplies

If a business supplies goods and services that are zero-rated or exempt from VAT, invoices that include these items must show this fact.

The zero-rated or exempt items should clearly show that there is no VAT payable, and the value of the items must be shown separately.

Invoices that are for **only** zero-rated or exempt supplies are not VAT invoices.

simplified invoices – supplies of less than £250

If the VAT-inclusive amount charged is £250 or less, a **simplified invoice** may be issued. This type of invoice must show:

■ a unique sequential invoice number

■ the supplier's name, address, and VAT registration number

■ the time of supply (tax point)

■ a description that identifies the goods or services

- the rate of VAT charged per item (if the item is exempt or zero-rated the invoice should make it clear that there is no VAT on this item)

- the total amount payable for each VAT rate, **including** VAT

It should be noted that a simplified invoice cannot include any exempt supplies.

modified invoices

A modified invoice is similar to a full VAT invoice, but it also includes the price of the products inclusive of VAT. A modified invoice is only issued for goods and services totalling more than £250 that include VAT taxable products.

A modified invoice can only be issued if the customer agrees to the invoice including product prices and total amounts including VAT.

Modified invoices are generally issued by retailers selling products direct to customers rather than to other businesses.

situations where VAT invoices are not needed

There are a number of situations where VAT invoices are not compulsory:

- where the buyer is not registered for VAT (although they must be given one if they ask)

- where the seller is a retailer (although a customer can ask for one)

- where the item is a free sample of something that is normally subject to VAT

- if the purchaser is on a **self-billing** system (ie the purchaser issues the invoice and sends it with the payment)

pro-forma invoice

A **pro-forma invoice** is a document issued by a seller offering goods at a certain price and inviting the buyer to send a payment in return for which the goods will then be supplied and invoiced in the normal way.

This is a common arrangement when a seller does not want to sell on credit – because there may be a credit risk – and so wants payment up front.

A pro-forma invoice (shown on the next page) may well look exactly like an invoice, but because it does not relate to a firm sale, **cannot be used as evidence to reclaim input tax**. Pro-forma invoices should be clearly marked 'THIS IS NOT A VAT INVOICE'. If a sale results from a pro-forma invoice, a separate invoice (VAT invoice) should then be issued.

PRO-FORMA INVOICE

SPICER STATIONERY
45 High Street
Mereford MR1 3TR
Tel 010903 443851
VAT Reg 422 8371 78

R M Electrical Ltd
56 High Street
Mereford MR5 8UH

13 May 20-5

Your ref Purchase Order 2934234

45 x A4 Box files (burgundy) @ £4.99 each	£224.55
VAT @ 20%	£44.91
TOTAL PAYABLE	£269.46

THIS IS NOT A VAT INVOICE.

A VAT invoice will be issued on receipt of the amount in full.

VAT receipt

Another document issued by VAT-registered businesses is the **VAT receipt**. You may have heard the question 'Do you want a VAT receipt?' when you fill up with fuel. People claiming the cost of fuel as a business expense will want a VAT receipt because the business may want to reclaim the VAT on the fuel.

VAT receipts are not always issued by VAT-registered retailers, but a customer can demand one, particularly if business expenses are involved.

A valid VAT receipt needs to show the following details:

- the name, address and VAT registration number of the retailer
- items charged at different VAT rates listed separately

The VAT receipt shown below is for petrol and milk bought at a supermarket.

Study the format of the receipt and note the separate listing and coding (A and D) of the milk (zero-rated) and the petrol (standard-rated).

name and address of supplier ➡	SAINSCO SUPERMARKETS PLC
	Nottingham NG1 3GF
VAT registration number ➡	VAT Number 3436675241

Your operator today is NINA
08/04/20-6 at 04.03 pm
Shift 4956
Transaction number 05554522 Till No 3

details of purchases	FRESH MILK	£1.53	A
	Pump 9: Unleaded		
	43.34 L @ 119.9	£53.06	D
	TOTAL	£54.59	
	PAID by VISA	£54.59	
	ICC 412934******4673		

	VAT Rate	Net Price	VAT	Gross Price
breakdown of VAT charged at zero and standard rates	A 0.0%	1.53	0.00	1.53
	D 20%	44.22	8.84	53.06

POINTS CARD
Points accumulated   3030
Points this transaction   645
Total Points   3675

THANK YOU FOR SHOPPING AT SAINSCO

VAT CALCULATIONS

In this section we look some of the main VAT calculations that need to be carried out. These include:

■ calculating VAT at different rates

■ the rules for rounding of VAT amounts

■ calculating the VAT content of a figure which contains VAT

■ calculating VAT after a discount is offered on an invoice

automatic calculation of VAT

Calculation of VAT at various rates on invoices and receipts is a straightforward matter. Most businesses now use accounting **software packages** which automatically calculate the VAT that is included in a purchase or sales invoice. However, it is important to remember that the correct rate of VAT must be coded for each invoice to ensure that the correct VAT rate is applied. Electronic tills in retail businesses will also be able to calculate the VAT on a sale automatically as the barcode, or produce code, will identify what it is and what rate of VAT is applicable.

VAT rounding

When you are calculating VAT manually, the problem of '**rounding**' arises. For example, if your calculator works out VAT due of £60.4567, what is the correct VAT amount in £s and pence?

HMRC allows businesses and other organisations to round down the **total** amount of VAT payable shown on an invoice or receipt to the nearest whole penny, so the total VAT due of £60.4567 would be shown as £60.45. This is different from the common method of rounding **up or down** to the nearest penny.

However, where a business uses accounting software that automatically calculates VAT on every line, for example a retailer, it will calculate the VAT separately for each line of goods or services. In this case each line should be numerically rounded up or down to the nearest 0.1 pence, ie 74.63 pence would be rounded to 74.6 pence, and 74.68 pence would be rounded to 74.7 pence.

Note: in the assessment for this unit you will be given instruction as to how to round figures if this is appropriate.

calculating VAT included in the total

As we've seen earlier in this chapter, sometimes you may have to deal with an invoice or receipt which quotes a figure including VAT at a certain rate, but does not separately identify the VAT amount included.

Let us take an example of a receipt or invoice for £24 for some stationery. This includes the cost of the stationery (100%) and also the VAT (at the standard rate of 20%). Therefore, the total amount equates to 120% of the cost price before VAT is added on.

The formula to use in this case is:

$$\frac{the\ total\ amount\ which\ includes\ VAT}{(100\% + VAT\%)} \times VAT\%$$

Applying this formula to the total figure of £24.00, the calculation is:

$$\frac{£24}{120\%} \times 20\% = a\ VAT\ content\ of\ £4.00$$

Therefore, the £24.00 total is made up of a cost price of £20.00 plus VAT of £4.00 (£20.00 is £24.00 minus £4.00).

the VAT fraction

Another way of working out the VAT included in a total amount is to multiply the whole amount by the 'VAT fraction'. This is $\frac{1}{6}$ for the current standard VAT rate of 20% (ie 20% / 120% = $\frac{1}{6}$). In practice, for the 20% VAT rate, all you have to do is to divide the whole amount which includes VAT by 6.

The calculation for the amount of £24 is:

$$£24.00 \div 6 = £4.00\ VAT.$$

It's worth noting that the $\frac{1}{6}$ VAT fraction only works for a VAT rate of 20%. If the VAT rate is different, the fraction will be different.

For example the VAT fraction for reduced rate VAT of 5%, is $\frac{1}{21}$. The reduced rate VAT can be found by dividing the total amount (including VAT) by 21.

The current VAT fractions are published in the HMRC VAT Guide.

DISCOUNTS

trade discount and VAT

HMRC requires that VAT is calculated on the invoiced amount after any **trade discount** has been deducted. For example, if you study the invoice on the next page, you will notice that a 10% trade discount has been applied before the VAT is calculated.

prompt payment discounts and VAT

The treatment of VAT after deduction of **prompt payment discount** is more complicated. **Prompt payment discount** (also known as settlement discount) is a discount offered by the seller to encourage the buyer to pay straightaway, or in a short time after the invoice has been issued, rather than waiting until the due date specified on the invoice. In this case the invoice terms would include a phrase like:

'Settlement discount of 2.5% for payment within seven days'.

This means that the seller will take 2.5% off the net invoice price (ie the price before VAT) if it is settled within seven days of the invoice date.

Where a business offers a prompt payment discount (PPD) it must always account for VAT on the money the customer pays, ie what it actually received. Because the customer may or may not take the PPD, the business will not know how much it will receive until the payment is made.

There are two ways that a business can deal with prompt payment discounts, and the VAT-registered business must decide which of the alternatives to use and express this appropriately on its invoices.

alternative 1 – issuing a credit note

The invoice applies the normal rate of VAT to the value of the goods or service. If the customer pays early and takes advantage of the lower charge, a lower amount of VAT will be due to HMRC. The seller will then have to issue a credit note to the customer (including VAT) for the amount of the prompt payment discount.

alternative 2 – statement included on the invoice

If the seller does not wish to issue a credit note every time a customer takes advantage of a prompt payment discount, then the invoice will be for the full amount plus VAT. The invoice must include a statement giving the terms of the PPD and how much the customer should pay if it pays within the prompt payment period.

It should also include a statement that the customer can only recover the actual VAT amount paid to the supplier as input tax. HMRC recommends that the following standard statement is included on invoices where a prompt payment discount is offered:

'A discount of X% of the full price applies if the payment is made within Y days of the invoice date. No credit note will be issued. Following payment you must ensure you have only recovered the VAT actually paid.'

The invoice below, issued by Artix Supplies, offers the customer, HG Wells Limited, a prompt payment discount. In this example, Artix Supplies has chosen to use alternative 2 and include a statement on the invoice.

INVOICE   ARTIX SUPPLIES

Unit 15 Maddox Estate, Broadfield, BR7 4ER
Tel 01908 765314 Fax 01908 765951 Email sales@artix.co.uk
VAT Reg GB 0745 4672 76

invoice to

HG Wells Limited
45 Rainbow Arcade
Hunstanton, NR1 3RF

invoice no	787923
account	3993
your reference	47609
date/tax point	02 10 20-3

deliver to

as above

product code	description	quantity	price £	unit	total £	discount %	net £
45B	Goya paint brushes	100	2.36	each	236.00	10.00	212.40

terms

A discount of 2.5% of the full price applies if the payment is made within 7 days of the invoice date. No credit note will be issued. Following payment you must ensure you have only recovered the VAT actually paid.

goods total	212.40
VAT @ 20%	42.48
TOTAL	254.88

an invoice with 10% trade discount deducted and 2.5% prompt payment discount

TAX POINTS

The **tax point** of a taxable supply is the date that it is recorded as taking place for the purposes of the VAT Return

There are different ways of determining the tax point, and a business will need to ensure that it uses the correct tax point for each transaction so that it is recorded on the correct VAT Return.

The first point to note is that HMRC makes a distinction between the **basic tax point** and the **actual tax point**.

basic tax points

If a business supplies **goods**, the **basic tax point** is usually the date when:

- the business despatches the goods to the customer, or

- the customer collects them, or

- the supplier makes them available for the customer to use (eg if the supplier is assembling something on the customer's premises)

If a business supplies **services,** the **basic tax point** is:

- the date when the service is carried out

- normally taken as the date when all the work is completed

actual tax points

The rules for basic tax points can be set aside if an **actual tax point** is created.

actual tax point – 14 day rule

If a VAT invoice is issued **within 14 days** of the basic tax point (date of despatch/supply) the invoice date becomes the actual tax point, ie the later date.

For example, a business receives an order from a customer for standard VAT-rated goods. The goods are delivered to the customer on 10 January and an invoice is issued on 14 January. The customer pays the invoice on 22 January. Because the invoice is issued to the customer within 14 days of the date the goods were delivered, the tax point for this invoice is 14 January.

actual tax point – advance payments

If a business offers its customers the option to pay in advance, or requires them to do so, and a VAT invoice is issued or payment is received **before the basic tax point** (the supply of the goods or service), the **actual tax point** is the earlier of:

- the date a VAT invoice is issued
- the date the business receives the advance payment

The business will include the VAT on the advance payment on the VAT Return for the period in which the actual tax point for the payment occurs.

For example, on 23 April a customer orders a custom-made sofa from a shop that requires full payment in advance. A VAT invoice is raised on 23 April and the customer pays on 25 April. The sofa takes six weeks to manufacture and is delivered to the customer on 7 May. In this case the VAT invoice has been issued and the payment has been received before the goods are received (the basic tax point). Therefore, the actual tax point is the date the VAT invoice was issued.

actual tax point – deposits

If a customer put down a deposit to reserve an item, this deposit is a proportion of the total selling price that a customer pays before the business supplies the goods or services. The tax point for this deposit is the earlier of:

- the date a VAT invoice is issued for the deposit
- the date the deposit is received

The business will include the VAT on the deposit on the VAT Return for the period when the actual tax point for the deposit occurs.

The VAT on the balance is accounted for on the VAT Return for the period when the tax point for the balance occurs.

For example, on 8 February a customer books a venue for their wedding on 20 July. They paid a 20% deposit to secure the booking, and a VAT invoice for this amount was issued on 9 February. A VAT invoice for the remaining 80% was issued on 20 June and the customer paid it on the same day. In this situation the tax point for the deposit is 8 February, and the tax point for the balance is 20 June.

actual tax point – continuous supply

If a business supplies a service to a customer on a continuous basis over a period of time that is longer than one month, it may issue invoices regularly throughout that period. In this case a tax point is created every time an invoice is issued, or a payment is made, whichever happens first.

actual tax point – sale or return

Sometimes a customer will have an arrangement with a supplier where it only pays the supplier for goods that it actually sells, with any unsold goods being returned to the supplier. An example of this would be a book shop that agrees to buy books from a publisher by a new author on the basis that if the book does not prove popular it can return any unsold copies to the publisher. Goods supplied on a sale or return basis remain the property of the supplier until the customer indicates they intend to keep them. The tax point for goods on sale or return is the earlier of:

- the date the customer adopts the goods (ie indicates they will keep the goods)

- the date payment is made by the customer. However, the receipt of a deposit which is repayable if the goods are returned is **not** an indication of adoption

- 12 months from the date the goods were sent

actual tax point – payment by instalment

A business may allow a customer to pay for goods by instalments over an agreed period of time. The goods remain the property of the business until the full price is paid. This is known as a '**conditional sale**' – in other words, the business is saying 'the goods will be yours when you have finished paying for them; until then they remain our property'.

The basic tax point for a conditional sale is created when the goods are handed over to the customer. On that date a business should account for the VAT on the **full value** of the goods.

the importance of tax points

A business needs to account for VAT correctly for all these situations and will need to know how to determine the correct tax point for the VAT Return.

The principle of the tax point is important to the VAT-registered business:

- it results in a consistent and accurate method of recording VAT transactions

- it can help cash flow in a business – an early tax point helps a business purchasing goods because the input tax can be reclaimed earlier, eg for a purchase in the last week of a VAT quarter (a VAT accounting period of three months), rather than in the next week – this will make a three month (VAT quarter) difference in cash flow

The determination of tax points is also important when deciding on the eligibility of a business to join one of the special VAT Schemes. This is covered in more detail in Chapter 3.

■ A VAT-registered supplier selling goods or services will provide a VAT invoice to the buyer; this invoice must contain certain details laid down by HMRC and will document the output tax charged by the seller and the input tax that the buyer may be able to claim back.

■ Supplies charged at different VAT rates on an invoice must show as separate items, with all VAT rates and amounts shown separately.

■ There are certain variations on the type of invoice that may be used: if the amount of the invoice is less than £250 including VAT, a simplified (less detailed) invoice may be used which does not show the VAT amount separately. Businesses can issue modified invoices for supplies of more than £250 which show the price of the product both inclusive and exclusive of VAT.

■ Businesses can issue electronic invoices but this must be done in a secure format such as pdf. Advantages include: instant transfer to customers, rapid access and retrieval, reduced storage and postage costs, improved cash flow, more secure transfer, and easier dispute handling.

■ A pro-forma invoice (used to request payment in advance) is not classed as a VAT invoice.

■ Businesses accounting for VAT may need to carry out a variety of calculations when dealing with VAT documentation, including working out the VAT content of an amount which includes VAT, and calculating VAT after discounts.

■ When VAT-registered businesses complete a VAT Return they must ensure that the time of the supply of goods and services for tax purposes – the tax point – is accurately recorded as it can affect the timing of payment of output tax and claims for input tax.

full VAT invoice	an invoice issued by a VAT-registered supplier which must contain certain details, including: – a consecutive invoice number and the date (which is normally the tax point) – the seller's name and address – the seller's VAT registration number – the buyer's name and address – a description of the goods or services – unit price and quantity – cost before VAT, VAT amount, total amount – VAT rate and total of VAT
modified invoice	a VAT invoice issued by a business for supplies of more than £250 which shows the price of the product both inclusive and exclusive of VAT
simplified invoice	an invoice for £250 or less (including VAT) that does not show the VAT amount(s) separately
pro-forma invoice	issued by a supplier, for a buyer to pay for goods before they are supplied – this is not a VAT invoice
VAT receipt	a document issued for a cash sale, often by a retailer, which shows the name, address and VAT registration number of the supplier and the VAT amounts and rates of the goods or services sold
rounding rules	HMRC has specific rules on VAT rounding on invoices which must be applied either to the total invoice amount or to the individual items on the invoice
VAT fraction	the fraction used to work out the VAT content of an amount which contains VAT
tax point	the date on which the supply is recorded for the purposes of the VAT Return – normally the date of the invoice
basic tax point	the date on which the goods are sent or collected, or the service performed (also normally the invoice date)
actual tax point	any variation to the basic tax point, for example if advance payment is made, or the 14 day rule applied
14 day rule	if a VAT invoice is issued up to 14 days after the basic tax point, the date of issue is the tax point

Activities

2.1 A VAT invoice for goods sent by a seller to a buyer within the UK must contain the following items:

(a)	Invoice number, purchase order number, seller's name, seller's VAT registration number	
(b)	Invoice number, invoice date, buyer's name, buyer's VAT registration number	
(c)	Invoice number, amount of VAT charged, unit price, VAT rate	
(d)	Invoice number, seller's address, unit price, buyer's VAT registration number	

Which **one** of these options is correct?

2.2 If a VAT invoice for goods sent by a seller in the UK covers the sale of two items, one zero-rated and the other standard-rated, the invoice should:

(a)	Show the two items on separate lines of the invoice with separate VAT rates and separate VAT amounts	
(b)	Only show the VAT amount for the standard-rated item because there is no VAT charged on the zero-rated item	
(c)	Only show the standard-rated item because there is no need for a VAT invoice for a zero-rated supply	
(d)	Charge VAT at an average rate worked out by adding the two rates together and dividing the total by two	

Which **one** of these options is correct?

2.3 A simplified invoice can be used when:

(a)	The supplier is not registered for VAT	
(b)	The buyer is not registered for VAT	
(c)	The supplies are zero-rated and so no VAT is involved	
(d)	The amount involved is £250 or less, including VAT	

Which **one** of these options is correct?

2.4   You work in the Accounts Department of a local carpet store and a salesperson who is new to the job hands you a slip of paper, saying:

'Here's a VAT receipt for some petrol I bought on company business – I have been told to hand it in so that you can get the VAT back.'

State **two** reasons why this cannot be used to reclaim VAT.

```
ASCO SUPERMARKETS PLC
     Liverpool LP5 4FT

Your operator today is JAMIE
13/05/20-6 at 12.03 pm
Shift 986
Transaction number 9479474 Till No 5

Bread rolls (six pack)              £1.25

Pump 9: Unleaded
35.90 L @ 129.9                    £46.63

TOTAL                             £47.88

PAID by VISA                      £47.88
ICC 412848******3756


POINTS CARD
Points accumulated        2056
Points this transaction    430
Total Points              2486

THANK YOU FOR SHOPPING AT ASCO
```

2.5   A pro-forma invoice is issued by a business selling goods so that:

(a)	The buyer can use it to claim back the input VAT on the goods	
(b)	The buyer can deduct prompt payment discount if payment is made within seven days	
(c)	The buyer can send a payment in advance to obtain the goods	
(d)	The buyer can avoid paying the VAT normally due on the goods	

Which **one** of these options is correct?

2.6 You work in the Accounts Department of a local business and are handed a receipt for payment for some stationery costing £23.44. There is no VAT amount shown on the receipt because the shop which sold the goods claimed that their till did not 'show VAT' as it was already included in all their prices. The current rate of VAT is 20%. You work out the VAT content to be:

(a)	£3.90	
(b)	£3.91	
(c)	£4.68	
(d)	£19.53	

Which **one** of these options is correct?

2.7 Decide which of the following is the basic tax point for a supplier selling goods.

(a)	The date the customer orders the goods	
(b)	The date the goods are sent to the customer	
(c)	The date the customer pays for the goods	
(d)	The date the next VAT Return is completed by the supplier	

Which **one** of these options is correct?

2.8 Gerome has ordered a pizza oven from Paolo's Pizza Limited and paid the invoiced amount of £500 plus VAT, in full. There is an eight-week delay before the oven will be delivered; however, to secure the item Gerome has had to pay the full amount in advance.

What is the actual tax point for Gerome's advance payment to Paolo's Pizza Limited?

(a)	The date of the payment	
(b)	The date of the VAT invoice	
(c)	The date that Gerome receives the goods	
(d)	The date Paolo's Pizza Limited complete its next VAT Return	

Which **one** of these options is correct?

2.9   If a business supplies a service to a customer on a continuous basis over period of a year, and invoices at various points during the 12-month period, when is a tax point created?

(a)	Once, at the end of the year	
(b)	Once, at the beginning of the year	
(c)	Every time an invoice is issued, or a payment is made, whichever is first	
(d)	Each time the business submits a VAT Return	

Which **one** of these options is correct?

2.10   Saoirse runs a small painting and decorating business. She orders brushes and paints from one of her suppliers. She receives a pro-forma invoice on 14 October and pays for the goods on 19 October. She collects the goods from the supplier on 25 October. She receives a VAT invoice dated 26 October by email which she does not open until 27 October.

What is the tax point for this invoice?

(a)	26 October	
(b)	25 October	
(c)	19 October	
(d)	14 October	

Which **one** of these options is correct?

2.11   Leximus Ltd delivers goods to a customer on 7 April and issues an invoice on 8 April for £1,620 including standard rate VAT at 20%. The customer paid the invoice on 15 April.

(a)   What is the tax point for this transaction?

7 April	
8 April	
15 April	
30 April	

Which **one** of these options is correct?

(b)   If Leximus Ltd offers a prompt payment discount of 5% when amounts are paid within 10 days, how much VAT will be recorded for this transaction if the customer pays promptly and takes the discount?

£ [   ]

3 Inputs and outputs and special schemes

this chapter covers...

This chapter describes further aspects of inputs and outputs, and input tax and output tax. It explains why it is important to get the timing of these inputs and outputs correct for the completion of the VAT Return. The specific areas covered include:

■ *the difference between input VAT and output VAT*

■ *the different rates of VAT*

■ *the difference between zero-rated supplies and exempt supplies when it comes to reclaiming input tax*

■ *the subject of partial exemption, which is where a business supplies both taxable goods or services and also exempt goods or services and so cannot normally reclaim all the input tax paid*

■ *the way in which businesses should account for VAT on business entertainment*

■ *how to deal with the input VAT on assets for private use*

■ *what is meant by blocked inputs for VAT purposes*

■ *the VAT situation which relates to the sale and purchase of cars and vans, reclaiming VAT paid on fuel used by cars and the need to pay fuel scale charges*

This chapter then explains how imports and exports of goods and services are treated for VAT purposes.

Lastly, this chapter describes the various special schemes for payment of VAT, including the annual accounting scheme, the flat rate scheme, and the cash accounting scheme.

OUTPUT VAT AND INPUT VAT – SOME REVISION

output VAT and input VAT – definitions

Input tax is the VAT a business is charged on its business purchases and expenses.

Output tax is the VAT that is due to HMRC on supplies of goods or services made by a business.

output VAT and input VAT – the rates

The current rates of VAT are:

- **standard rate** 20%
- **reduced rate** 5%
- **zero rate** 0%

These rates of VAT (apart from zero rate) can change from time to time.

output VAT and input VAT – the calculation

The VAT amount due to HMRC from a VAT-registered business is calculated in the VAT Return as: **output tax less input tax**.

Therefore, HMRC will want to ensure that a VAT-registered business:

- **charges** the correct amount of output tax – this is comparatively straightforward as it is calculated by applying the appropriate percentage rate to the taxable supply of goods or services
- **claims** the correct amount of input tax (and no more than the correct amount) to offset against the output VAT it charges – here the regulations are more complex, as we will see in this chapter

Businesses must also consider the **timing of a claim** for input tax. The buyer of goods or services will want to claim for any input VAT incurred as soon as possible, as this will help the cash flow of the business.

The timing of the claim for input tax is normally based on the **tax point** of the transaction which we covered in the last chapter. In most cases this is the date the invoice is issued for the supply of the goods or services.

There are variations on this timing, through a variation in the tax point and also through VAT Special Schemes, which are covered later in this chapter.

ZERO-RATED AND EXEMPT SUPPLIES

Zero-rated goods and services, eg food and children's clothes, are chargeable to output VAT, but at zero per cent, so no VAT is charged. A supplier of zero-rated goods and services, that is registered for VAT, will be able to reclaim input VAT spent on business purchases and expenses. Therefore, when a supplier of zero-rated goods and services completes a VAT Return, the calculation of output VAT (zero) minus input VAT results in a negative figure. This means that HMRC will then owe the business this amount and will make a VAT refund. This will normally be sent electronically direct to the bank account of the business, giving a useful boost to its cash flow.

Goods and services that are VAT-exempt, for example providers of educational courses and healthcare, are treated differently. Businesses that only supply exempt goods and services are not able to register for VAT, and so will never be able to reclaim any input VAT. This means that the input VAT incurred becomes part of their expenses.

In conclusion:

- suppliers of **zero-rated** goods and services should register for VAT and are able to reclaim input VAT that they pay on business supplies

- suppliers of **VAT-exempt** goods and services cannot reclaim the input VAT that they pay on business purchases

TAXABLE AND EXEMPT SUPPLIES – PARTIAL EXEMPTION

The VAT regulations state that, normally, if a business is registered for VAT and makes:

- **some** supplies that are VAT-exempt and

- **some** supplies that are taxable (eg standard-rated)

the business will not be able to reclaim the input VAT it has paid on the purchases relating to the exempt supplies it has made.

A business in this situation is referred to as **partially exempt**.

However, HMRC states that if the amount of VAT incurred relating to exempt supplies is below a certain amount (known as the '**de minimis**' limit), input VAT can be recovered in full, including the proportion relating to the exempt supplies.

We will now explain both of these situations.

partial exemption – how to work out the input tax

If a business makes both taxable and exempt supplies and has to pay input tax on purchases that relate to both kinds of supply, the business will be classified as **'partly exempt'**.

Unless the business qualifies under the 'de minimis' rules (see next page), it will have to calculate how much of its input tax is recoverable.

The following examples illustrates this.

Speakeasy Ltd, a business that provides educational courses and podcasts, has annual taxable sales above the annual VAT registration threshold, so is VAT-registered. It has two main products:

■ intensive English language courses for overseas students studying in the UK – these courses are VAT-exempt under HMRC regulations because they are providing an educational service

■ the 'Speakeasy' series of downloadable foreign language podcasts which are available to download by UK consumers – these are standard-rated for VAT under HMRC regulations because they are taxable supplies

How does this affect Speakeasy Ltd's VAT Return?

output VAT is relatively straightforward:

■ it is only charged on the podcasts, which are standard-rated

■ it is not charged on the language courses because they are VAT-exempt

input VAT is more complicated:

■ VAT charged on purchases and expenses directly related to providing the language courses **cannot be reclaimed as input tax** because it relates to the provision of exempt supplies, ie the language courses

■ VAT charged on purchases and expenses directly related to the downloadable podcasts **can be claimed as input tax** because it relates to standard-rated supplies, ie the downloads that Speakeasy sells

The problem is that there are also some purchases and expenses which **cannot be directly allocated to either courses or podcasts**, for example telephone bills and administration costs.

The input tax charged on these supplies is known as **'residual input tax'**. **Some of this input tax** may be recovered according to the proportion that taxable supplies (the podcasts) make up of its total supplies.

So, if Speakeasy's total supplies are £120,000, and £36,000 of these are taxable (ie the sale of the downloadable podcasts), the percentage of the residual input VAT that can be claimed is:

$$\frac{£36,000 \times 100}{£120,000} = 30\%$$

The remaining 70% of the input VAT cannot be claimed as input tax, and must be treated as a business expense.

partial exemption – the 'de minimis' limit

The **'de minimis' limit** allows a business to recover **all** the input VAT charged on taxable **and exempt** purchases and expenses, provided the total value of that input tax is less than a set amount – ie the 'de minimis' limit.

HMRC is allowing businesses that sell a mix of taxable supplies and VAT-exempt supplies to avoid having to carry out calculations for partial exemption described above. Instead, they are allowed to include all the input tax related to their taxable and exempt supplies.

The phrase 'de minimis' means 'so small that it is really not worth bothering about'.

The de minimis test that allows businesses to recover all input tax is that input tax relating to exempt supplies must be:

■ no more than £625 per month

■ less that 50% of total input VAT in the period

This is illustrated by the following example.

A business supplies a mix of exempt and VATable goods. The input tax in the year relating to exempt supplies is £5,940 and the input tax relating to VATable goods is £7,000. The question is whether this business can claim partial exemption under the de minimis limit.

First, we check whether, on average, input VAT on exempt goods is less than £625 per month. £5,940 divided by 12 months is an average of £495 per month, so it is.

Second, we need to check whether the input tax on the exempt supplies is less than 50% of the total input tax for the year.

Total input VAT for the year is £5,940 + £7,000 = £12,940

$$\frac{£5,940 \times 100}{£12,940} = 46\% \text{ relating to exempt supplies}$$

This means that the business complies with the de minimis test and can, therefore, treat its exempt input tax as if it were taxable input tax and recover it in full.

BLOCKED INPUT VAT

It is important to understand that businesses can only claim back VAT which has been charged on costs and expenses that are actually **business expenses**.

If a business uses goods or services partly for business purposes and partly for non-business purposes, it must identify which of them relate to the business and which are non-business expenses when calculating a claim for input VAT.

Blocked expenses are those expenses on which a business cannot reclaim input VAT.

business entertainment

HMRC states that a business **cannot recover input tax that relates to business entertainment** – ie it is **blocked.** Examples of business entertainment are:

- provision of food and drink, eg meals in restaurants
- provision of accommodation, eg in hotels
- theatre and concert tickets
- entry to sporting events and facilities
- use of facilities such as villa and aircraft for the purpose of entertaining

The exception to this is where input tax relates to entertaining overseas customers, ie not UK or Isle of Man customers, which is allowable.

employee entertainment

Business entertainment should not be confused with **employee entertainment.** If a business provides entertainment to reward employees for good work, or to improve staff morale, this is considered to be for business purposes and is not blocked. Therefore, the input VAT can be reclaimed. Examples of staff entertainment are seasonal staff parties and staff outings.

mixed entertaining

When a business entertains employees and clients together, it may be able to claim back the proportion of the input VAT that does not relate to clients, customers, potential customers or suppliers of the business – ie what relates to staff entertaining can be reclaimed.

For example, if a business entertains employees and customers together, it may be able to reclaim the VAT on the proportion relating to employee entertainment.

However, none of the VAT can be reclaimed if the sole purpose of the activity is to entertain the non-employee(s). For example, if several members of staff take one client out for a round of golf, none of the VAT can be claimed.

VEHICLES AND VAT

car and van purchase

Businesses are not normally permitted to reclaim the input VAT when they buy a **car**, ie the input VAT is **blocked.** However, they are able to reclaim all the input VAT if:

■ the car will be used wholly for business purposes and is not available for private use by employees or family – not even for driving to work

■ the business is a taxi business, a driving instructor or provides self-drive hire cars

■ the business is a car dealer, and the car will be part of its inventory (stock) that it intends to sell within the next 12 months

A business can reclaim all the VAT on vehicle repairs and maintenance as long as:

■ the business pays for the work

■ there is some business use of the vehicle

Businesses can reclaim the input VAT paid on the purchase of **commercial vehicles** such as **vans**, **lorries,** or **tractors** in the normal way.

leasing a car

If a business leases or hires a car, it can usually claim 50% of the VAT on the leasing payments.

For example, Merix Ltd leases a Mercedes for its finance director. The monthly leasing cost is £651.60, including VAT at standard rate.

Using the VAT fraction, the VAT included in the leasing payment is calculated as: $\frac{1}{6}$ x £651.60 = £108.60.

Merix Ltd can claim 50% of the input VAT: 50% x £108.60 = £54.30

car and van sale

If a business was not able to reclaim the input VAT on the original purchase of a car which was bought, it cannot charge any VAT when the car is sold.

If a business such as a driving school wishes to sell a car for which it was originally able to reclaim the input VAT when it was bought, it will have to charge VAT on the full selling price of the car and also issue a VAT invoice to the buyer if it is VAT-registered, if it asks for one.

reclaiming VAT on road fuel

Businesses commonly buy, or lease, cars for use by their employees. Often known as 'company cars', employees are usually allowed to use them for private travel as well as business use.

If a business pays for road fuel used by employees, there are four different ways in which it can deal with the VAT charged on the fuel:

- if **all** the fuel is used only for business purposes (which does not include driving to work), the business can reclaim **all** of the input VAT charged

- the business does not need to reclaim any of the input VAT on fuel – this can be a useful option if the mileage of the vehicle is very low, and/or if the fuel is used for both business and private motoring. If a business chooses this option, it must apply it to **all** company vehicles, including commercial vehicles such as vans or lorries

- if the fuel is used for business purposes and for private motoring, the business can reclaim only the VAT that relates to fuel used for business mileage – this means that the business (and the employee) needs to keep detailed records of business and private mileage

- if the fuel is used for business purposes and for private motoring, the business can reclaim all of the VAT charged and then pay a separate **fuel scale charge** (see next section)

fuel scale charge

Businesses that purchase fuel which will be used for both business and private motoring can account for VAT by:

- reclaiming all the VAT charged, and

- paying a **fuel scale charge** to HMRC

The fuel scale charge is a charge on the CO_2 (carbon dioxide) emissions of vehicles: the higher the emissions, the greater the effect on the environment, and the higher the fuel scale charge. To some extent, this charge has a political agenda as it means that the government can be seen to be environmentally friendly and supporting sustainability because it is effectively taxing atmospheric pollution.

If a business opts to account for private usage of fuel by paying the fuel scale charge, there is a simple calculation tool on the HMRC section of the government website. Before starting the calculation, the business will need to know the CO_2 emissions figure for the vehicle, which is available in the logbook.

Although the tool on the HMRC website is available to automatically calculate the fuel scale charge for each vehicle, you need to be able to understand this calculation and carry it out yourself in your assessment. The process to calculate the fuel scale charge is:

- select the period (from 1 May to 30 April) the business wants to calculate the fuel scale charge for

- decide the length of the accounting period for which the fuel scale charge is being calculated ie monthly (1 month), quarterly (3 months) or annually (12 months)

- use the vehicle's CO_2 emissions figure to decide which band it falls into

- finally, use the table on the next page to identify the fuel scale charge for the vehicle

- if the business changes a car during the accounting period, then the fuel scale charge will need to be apportioned

Note: Where the CO_2 emissions figure is not a multiple of 5, the figure is rounded down to the next multiple of 5 to determine the level of the fuel scale charge.

Let's use the example of a business that submits quarterly VAT Returns and has a vehicle with CO_2 emissions of 153g/km. Using the table on the next page, the VAT inclusive amount of fuel scale charge to be included in its VAT Return for the quarter ended 31 March 2024 will be £368. The VAT amount to be added to output tax on the VAT Return is calculated as:

$$\frac{£368 \times 20}{120} = £61.33$$

The VAT exclusive amount is £306.67 (£368 – £61.33).

Fuel scale charge rates tend to increase every year. 'Gas guzzling' cars can generally be charged a rate which is significantly more than three times as much as the charge for a low-emission vehicle.

Once the fuel scale charge has been calculated for all cars with an element of private use, the VAT on this charge must be included in the business's VAT Control account. It will then be included in the VAT Return, which is covered in Chapter 4.

fuel scale charges for the period 1 May 2023 to 30 April 2024

Description of vehicle: vehicle's CO_2 emissions figure	VAT inclusive consideration for a 12 month prescribed accounting period (£)	VAT inclusive consideration for a 3 month prescribed accounting period (£)	VAT inclusive consideration for a 1 month prescribed accounting period (£)
120 or less	737	183	61
125	1,103	276	91
130	1,179	293	97
135	1,250	312	103
140	1,327	331	110
145	1,398	349	115
150	1,474	368	122
155	1,545	386	128
160	1,622	405	134
165	1,693	423	140
170	1,769	441	146
175	1,840	459	152
180	1,917	478	159
185	1,988	497	164
190	2,064	515	171
195	2,135	534	178
200	2,212	552	183
205	2,283	571	190
210	2,359	588	195
215	2,430	607	202
220	2,507	626	208
225 or more	2,578	644	214

ASSETS WITH PRIVATE USE

If a business buys an asset that is solely for business use, it can claim 100% of the VAT that it pays on the purchase as input tax. However, if the business buys an asset which will be used part of the time by the business and part by the owner, or an employee, this is known as a **mixed use asset**. Input VAT on the purchases of a mixed use asset should be apportioned to reflect the use of the asset, with only the proportion relating to the business use claimed as input VAT by the business.

For example, Sam, a VAT-registered plumber, buys a computer for £3,000 plus VAT. He has worked out that he will use the computer 70% of the time for work and the remaining 30% of the time, his son will use it for college work. Sam can claim 70% of the input VAT on his VAT Return, ie £420 (£3,000 x 20% x 70%).

HMRC has no set method for how to apportion the VAT, but it does state that the method should be 'fair and reasonable.' In the example, Sam should be able to justify why he has used the 70:30 split should HMRC ask for details.

Clearly, if a business purchases an asset that is solely for personal use it must not reclaim any of the input tax.

IMPORTS AND EXPORTS

The VAT rules relating to imports and exports differ depending on whether they relate to goods or services. We will look at goods first, because these are more straightforward, and then look at the rules that relate to services.

import of goods

So far, we have dealt with VAT as it affects business transactions within the UK. However, VAT must also be accounted for in dealings with businesses overseas. Since VAT is charged on supplies of goods and services made in the UK, it also needs to be charged on supplies of goods and services which are made abroad, to avoid giving overseas suppliers an advantage over UK suppliers.

The basic principle, which applies to exports and imports, is that because VAT is a tax on imported goods and some services, it is paid, where appropriate, by the importer and is treated as an input tax.

If you import goods into the UK, you may have to pay import VAT on these goods. The rate of VAT on goods that are imported is normally the **same rate** as if they had been supplied in the UK.

Most VAT-registered businesses account for import VAT on their VAT

Return by using **postponed VAT accounting** which allows the business to declare import VAT and reclaim it as input tax on the same VAT Return.

The business can reclaim the VAT incurred on the imported goods as input tax subject to the normal rules. We will see at how this is done when we look at completing the VAT Return in Chapter 4.

Postponed VAT accounting has significant cashflow benefits. Rather than paying the VAT upfront when goods are imported and then recovering it later, a business can delay payment by declaring and recovering import VAT on the same VAT Return. You will see how this works in Chapter 4 which covers the VAT Return.

Alternatively, a business can choose to pay import VAT when the goods enter the country rather than using postponed VAT accounting. If this option is chosen, the VAT incurred on the imported goods can be reclaimed as normal input tax. To claim input tax the business will need the import VAT statement as evidence.

If a UK business is **not registered for UK VAT**, it will still have to pay the import VAT when the imports enter the UK, but it will not be able to reclaim it.

export of goods

Because VAT is a tax on goods used in the UK, businesses do not charge VAT on goods that are **exported** outside the UK.

Instead, goods that are **exported** can normally be zero-rated, as long as the supplier retains documentary evidence of the export and all laws are obeyed. A business must not zero-rate the goods if the overseas customer asks for them to be delivered to a UK address.

place of supply

For VAT purposes it is important to know the place of supply of goods or services, as this is the place where VAT will be charged and paid.

For goods, it is straightforward to determine the place of supply of goods as this is the country where the goods come from.

The place of supply for services is more complicated. The general rule for most supplies of services is shown in the table below.

Supply is being made to a:	The place of supply is treated as:
business customer	the place where the customer is located
non-business customer	the place where the supplier is located

export of services

Where a UK business supplies a service to a business located overseas, this is outside the scope of UK VAT. However, the UK business must include the net sales in the VAT Return with its other net sales.

If a UK business provides a service to a non-business customer, the supplier charges UK VAT on the services as if the customer is located in the UK.

import of services–reverse charge

If a business in the UK buys services from a supplier in another country, depending on the circumstances, the business will have to account for the VAT itself. This is called the '**reverse charge**'. Where this applies, the business acts as if it is both the supplier and the customer.

It charges itself the VAT and then claims this back as input tax subject to the normal rules. In most cases the two amounts will be the same and cancel each other out.

reverse charge step-by-step

- treat the supply as if the business is supplying itself

- treat the supply of the service as a sale **and** a purchase

- on the VAT Return include the VAT in output VAT, and in input VAT

- include the net cost with other net sales and purchases

SPECIAL SCHEMES

HMRC has a number of special schemes which vary the way in which VAT is collected. They include the annual accounting scheme, the flat rate scheme, and the cash accounting scheme.

These schemes are described in the next few pages.

ANNUAL ACCOUNTING SCHEME FOR VAT

This scheme enables businesses to make one **annual** VAT Return.

The main features of the scheme are:

- a VAT-registered business can join the scheme if its maximum estimated taxable turnover for the next 12 months is no more than **£1.35 million**

- taxable turnover includes supplies at standard, reduced or zero-rated VAT, but excludes the VAT itself, and the sale of any capital assets, eg a car

- if annual taxable turnover goes over £1.35 million, the trader can continue on this scheme until its estimated taxable turnover for the next annual accounting year reaches **£1.6 million** at which point the business **must** leave the scheme
- the trader must either:
  - pay 90% of its estimated annual VAT payment based on its previous year's VAT Return, by nine equal monthly interim payments starting in the fourth month of the VAT year, ie nine payments on account which are 10% of its previous total VAT payable, or
  - pay three interim payments, each equal to 25% of the previous year's VAT liability, or 25% of the likely annual VAT liability if the business has been VAT-registered for less than 12 months. This is payable in months 4, 7 and 10 of the annual accounting period
- the trader must then submit its annual VAT Return electronically within two months of the end of the VAT year, and pay the balance due, or claim a repayment
- all payments must be made electronically
- a business can voluntarily withdraw from the annual accounting scheme for VAT at any time by writing to HMRC; HMRC will confirm when the business can leave. From this point the business must account for VAT in the usual way
- the annual accounting scheme **can be operated in conjunction with the flat rate scheme for VAT, or the cash accounting scheme for VAT** (both of which are covered in the following pages), **but not both**
- If a business that operates the annual accounting scheme is taken over as a going concern, the acquiring business must assess the use of the annual accounting scheme and calculate the expected and combined turnover of the new business. If this is expected to exceed £1.6 million, the business must immediately cease to use the scheme.

The timing of the payments that should be made under the annual accounting scheme for VAT is summarised in the table below.

Month	1	2	3	4	5	6	7	8	9	10	11	12	13	14
Payments (9 interim)				1	2	3	4	5	6	7	8	9		10
Payments (3 interim)				1			2			3				4

advantages of annual accounting scheme

- the scheme helps the business smooth out its cash flow by paying a set amount each month, or quarter

- the business only needs to submit one VAT Return each year, instead of the four required under the standard VAT scheme

- the business is allowed two months, instead of one, to complete and submit its online annual VAT Return and, if necessary, make the balancing payment

- the business can align its VAT year with the end of its business tax year to simplify its year-end processes

disadvantages of annual accounting scheme

- if the business regularly reclaims VAT (for example if it supplies zero-rated goods) it will only get one repayment of VAT each year

- if the business's turnover decreases, its interim VAT payments may be higher than they would have been under standard VAT accounting as they will be based on the previous year's VAT liability

FLAT RATE SCHEME FOR VAT

The **flat rate scheme** is very different from normal VAT schemes in which input VAT and output VAT are identified and recorded, resulting either in net VAT being paid over to HMRC, or reclaimed (if tax on expenses [inputs] is greater than VAT on sales [outputs]).

- a business using the flat rate scheme does not have to identify and record every single VAT transaction in order to calculate the net amount of VAT due. Instead, it applies a **flat percentage rate** to its total turnover for the VAT period (including VAT and exempt supplies) to calculate the amount of VAT due.

- the business must still issue VAT invoices to its customers, including the appropriate rate of VAT

- the business cannot claim input VAT – this is taken into account in the flat rate percentage

- The flat rate varies depending on the business sector. Some common examples are shown in the table on the next page.

type of business	flat rate
retailers of food and newspapers	4%
sports or recreation	8.5%
photography	11%
entertainment	12.5%
agricultural services	11%
accounting and bookkeeping services	14.5%

- a business can join the flat rate scheme if its taxable turnover for the next 12 months is forecast to be less than £150,000

- a business operating the flat rate scheme must assess its taxable turnover annually. If its turnover in the previous 12 months, including VAT and exempt supplies, or its expected turnover for the next 12 months, exceeds £230,000 a year, the business must leave the scheme

- a business can voluntarily withdraw from the flat rate accounting scheme for VAT at any time by writing to HMRC; HMRC will confirm when the business can leave. From this point the business must account for VAT in the usual way and must wait 12 months if it wishes to re-join the scheme.

The calculation of flat rate VAT is simple.

For example, a bookkeeper with quarterly supplies (ie income from clients) of £24,000, including VAT, will use a flat rate of 14.5%. Their quarterly VAT liability is:

$$£24,000 \times 14.5\% = £3,480$$

A photography studio also with quarterly turnover £24,000 would have a VAT liability of:

$$£24,000 \times 11\% = £2,640$$

A **benefit of the flat rate scheme** is that a business in its first year of VAT registration gets a 1% reduction on its applicable flat rate percentage for the first 12 months of VAT registration. Consequently the photography studio, above, would apply a flat rate of 10% in its first year of registration and so would have a quarterly VAT liability of £2,400 (£24,000 x10%). In the second year of registration the percentage would increase to 11%.

It is important to remember that the flat rate is only used to calculate the amount of VAT owed to HMRC by the business, because an allowance is made for input tax in the percentage. The business **does not charge VAT at the flat rate,** but instead at the normal rate for the supplies. It will issue VAT invoices showing the normal VAT rate charged.

If supplies are **zero-rated** (for example, a business selling books) and the business normally reclaims VAT as inputs are higher than outputs, it should not use the flat rate scheme (unless it wants to give money away!).

limited cost business

A flat rate of 16.5% must be used by businesses that provide services but only incur minimal costs. Many of these limited cost businesses are self-employed, 'labour-only' businesses.

A business is classed as a 'limited cost business' if its expenditure on goods, including VAT, is less than either:

- 2% of its VAT inclusive turnover

- £1,000 a year (if its costs are more than 2%)

A business that falls into this category pays a flat rate of 16.5%, whatever business sector it operates in.

The flat rate scheme **can be operated with the annual accounting scheme**, which makes dealing with VAT much simpler for small businesses. Not only is VAT calculated as a basic percentage, it is also only calculated once a year.

If a business operating the flat rate scheme is taken over as a going concern, the acquiring business must assess the use of the flat rate scheme in the context of the expected and combined turnover of the new business. If this is expected to exceed £230,000 then the business must immediately cease to use the flat rate scheme.

capital expenditure under the flat rate scheme

If a business purchases a large **capital asset**, eg a computer, with an invoice value (including VAT) of £2,000 or more, it can claim the actual input VAT paid on this asset. If the business later sells the asset, it will have to charge VAT at the full rate and pay back the VAT it receives to HMRC. This extra VAT on purchases (inputs) and sales (outputs) will be recorded on the VAT Return, which is due quarterly (unless the flat rate scheme is operated in conjunction with the annual accounting scheme).

VAT records for the flat rate scheme

A business will need to keep the following records if it operates the flat rate scheme:

- the flat rate turnover for the VAT accounting period

- the flat rate percentage used

- the VAT calculated as due

- a VAT account – recording VAT paid under the scheme and any VAT involved in the purchase or sale of a capital asset

CASH ACCOUNTING SCHEME FOR VAT

The cash accounting scheme for VAT allows businesses to account for VAT on the basis of the date **payments** are received and made, rather than on the tax point for **invoices** issued and received.

So, under this scheme, rather than accounting for output tax on the date of the supply, a business will account for it if/when payment is received from the customer, which may be several months later.

This scheme helps traders who have to pay their suppliers promptly, but have to wait some time before receiving payment from customers.

It also provides automatic relief for VAT on bad debts: if the buyer does not ever pay, no output VAT is declarable (as it would be if VAT was assessable on tax point, rather than payment, date).

To qualify for the cash accounting scheme a business must:

- anticipate annual taxable turnover of £1.35 million or less – this includes taxable supplies at standard rate, reduced rate and zero rate, but excludes VAT itself and exempt supplies

- have a 'clean' VAT record – ie have made all VAT Returns on time, have no assessments for VAT evasion and no convictions for VAT fraud

Other aspects of the scheme are:

- a business can continue to operate the cash accounting scheme until its annual taxable turnover exceeds £1.6 million, at which point it must leave the scheme

- a business can also voluntarily withdraw from the cash accounting scheme for VAT at any time.

- if a business takes over a business operating the cash accounting scheme as a going concern, it must assess the expected, combined turnover. If this is expected to exceed £1.6 million, the business must immediately cease to operate the scheme.

When operating the cash accounting scheme, a business will continue to issue VAT invoices but will need to keep accounting records in a specific way:

- the tax point for payments in cash, by cheque, credit card, or bank transfer is always the transaction date (eg the date on the credit card voucher)

- invoices issued or received for any payments made in cash must be receipted and dated

The cash accounting scheme cannot be operated in conjunction with the flat rate scheme, but **can be operated with the annual accounting scheme**.

Chapter Summary

■   Input tax is the VAT a business is charged on its business purchases and expenses – it can often be reclaimed. Output tax is the VAT that is due to HMRC on supplies of goods or services made by a business.

■   Different types of taxable supplies of goods and services will be charged at a variety of different VAT rates. These include: standard rate, reduced rate and zero rate. VAT is not charged at any rate on exempt supplies.

■   The difference between zero-rated and exempt supplies is that suppliers who are VAT-registered and sell zero-rated supplies can reclaim input VAT, whereas sellers of VAT-exempt supplies cannot reclaim input VAT.

■   Partial exemption is where a supplier sells a mix of VAT-rated and exempt goods and services and has to calculate how much input tax it can reclaim on the basis of the amount of VAT-rated goods sold. The exception to this is where the amount of exempt input tax is insignificant and can be reclaimed anyway under the 'de minimis' rule.

■   Businesses can only reclaim input tax where the expense involved is a business expense. Business entertainment – eg free entertainment for UK customers – is not classed as a business expense and the input tax cannot be reclaimed. This is known as blocked input VAT. However, the VAT on entertainment of employees and overseas customers can be reclaimed.

■   The input VAT charged on vehicles bought by a business cannot be reclaimed unless the vehicle is solely used for business purposes. If a business sells a car on which no VAT was reclaimed, it will not have to charge VAT on the sale. Only 50% of input VAT on the costs of leasing a vehicle can be reclaimed, unless it is used solely for business purposes.

■   If a business buys fuel for vehicles which are only used for business purposes, it may reclaim the input VAT; if the vehicle is also used for private purposes the business may only reclaim all the VAT if it pays a fuel scale charge based on the vehicle's CO_2 emissions.

■   If a business buys an asset that will be used partly by the business and partly by the owner, or an employee, the input VAT should be apportioned to reflect the use of the asset. Only the business portion can be reclaimed.

■   If VAT-registered businesses buy and sell goods and services (imports and exports) from abroad. The VAT charge on imports of goods is normally at the UK VAT rate that would be charged if the goods were supplied in the UK. Businesses can delay payment of VAT on taxable imports using postponed VAT accounting. Exports of goods should be zero-rated. Imported services should apply the reverse charge. The VAT treatment for exported services depends on the place of supply and whether the services are supplied to a business or a non-business customer.

■   To help businesses that may be put at a disadvantage by the standard VAT scheme, HMRC has a number of special schemes for VAT, ie annual accounting scheme, flat rate scheme, and cash accounting scheme.

Key Terms	**partial exemption**	where a business makes both taxable and exempt supplies and has to calculate the amount of input tax it can reclaim, based on the extent of its taxable supplies
	'de minimis' limit	where the amount of input tax which relates to a supplier's exempt supplies – which the supplier could not normally reclaim – is so insignificant that HMRC allows the business to reclaim it
	business entertainment	entertainment provided free of charge to people who are not employees of a business – food, drink, accommodation, theatre, sport
	blocked expenses	expense of the business on which the input VAT cannot be reclaimed, ie it is blocked
	fuel scale charge	a charge based on the CO_2 emissions of a vehicle to account for the VAT on fuel for personal use of a company vehicle
	exports and imports	the sale and purchase of goods to/from business located abroad
	postponed VAT accounting	businesses declare the VAT on imports and reclaim the VAT on the same VAT Return, rather than paying the VAT when the goods arrive in the UK
	reverse charge	businesses that import services must treat the supply as a sale and a purchase, and include the VAT on the imported service as both output and input VAT on the VAT Return
	annual accounting scheme	a scheme which enables businesses (with annual taxable turnover of £1.35 million or less) to make VAT Returns annually rather than quarterly – VAT owing is paid in regular instalments and the VAT Return is due two months after the end of the VAT year
	flat rate scheme	a scheme which enables businesses with an annual taxable turnover of up to £150,000 to pay VAT at a flat percentage rate based on tax inclusive turnover

limited cost business

a business operating the flat rate scheme, with costs of goods that are less than either 2% of its turnover, or £1,000 a year (if its costs are more than 2% of turnover), must use a flat rate of 16.5% if it wishes to operate the flat rate scheme for VAT

cash accounting scheme

a scheme which allows businesses (with annual taxable turnover of £1.35 million or less) to account for VAT on the basis of payments received and made rather than the tax point on invoices received and issued; it provides automatic relief for VAT on bad debts

Activities

3.1 A business will be unable to reclaim input VAT if it supplies are:

(a)	Zero-rated	
(b)	Exempt	
(c)	Standard-rated	
(d)	Reduced-rated	

Which **one** of these options is correct?

3.2 A business that is partially exempt supplies:

(a)	Some goods that are zero-rated and some that are standard-rated	
(b)	Some goods that are zero-rated and some that are reduced-rated	
(c)	Some goods that are standard-rated and some that are exempt	
(d)	Some goods that are standard-rated and some that are reduced-rated	

Which **one** of these options is correct?

3.3 Residual input tax is the VAT that:

(a)	Is charged on costs and expenses that cannot definitely be attributed to standard-rated supplies or to exempt supplies	
(b)	Is charged on costs and expenses that have not been settled at the end of the VAT accounting period	
(c)	Is charged on costs and expenses that can definitely be attributed to standard-rated supplies or to zero-rated supplies	
(d)	Is charged on costs and expenses that have been settled before the due date in order to obtain prompt payment discount	

Which **one** of these options is correct?

3.4   A 'de minimis' limit is:

(a)	The amount set for the lowest rate of the fuel scale charge levied on very small cars	
(b)	The annual sales turnover limit set for registration for partial exemption	
(c)	The annual sales turnover limit set for VAT registration for a business making exempt supplies	
(d)	The limit set which enables a partially exempt business to reclaim input VAT paid on exempt supplies	

Which **one** of these options is correct?

3.5   Your business will be able to deduct input VAT on the VAT Return in the following circumstances:

(a)	You fill up your company car with fuel when driving home (no fuel scale charge is paid)	
(b)	You take a small group of customers for a night out at a local club	
(c)	You take a group of customers to an international rugby match	
(d)	You take your employees out for a celebratory meal	

Which **one** of these options is correct?

3.6   A business buying a car can deduct input VAT charged on the car when:

(a)	The car will be used by the Managing Director and his family	
(b)	The car is used by a salesperson for business trips only and is kept at the employee's home	
(c)	The business is a car hire firm, and the car will be hired out to customers	
(d)	The car is mostly used for business purposes but is occasionally used by employees at the weekend out of business hours	

Which **one** of these options is correct?

3.7   Bradbow Ltd provides a company car to its sales manager. The business has paid for all the car's fuel since it was purchased, including VAT at standard rate. The car has CO_2 emissions of 164 g/km.

Bradbow Ltd reclaims all the VAT on the fuel and accounts for private fuel used by the sales manager using the appropriate fuel scale charge. Which of these is the correct fuel scale charge for the VAT quarter ending 30 September 2023?

(a)	£134	
(b)	£405	
(c)	£423	
(d)	£1,622	

Which **one** of these options is correct?

3.8   Frownaway Ltd leases a car for its managing director. The monthly leasing cost is £478.50 plus VAT. How much of the input VAT on the leasing payment can Frownaway Ltd reclaim each month?

(a)	£95.70	
(b)	£79.75	
(c)	£47.85	
(d)	£39.88	

Which **one** of these options is correct?

3.9   The annual accounting scheme requires that:

(a)	The VAT Return has to be submitted every 12 months	
(b)	Taxable turnover must be at standard rate or at reduced rate	
(c)	The VAT payment only needs to be made to HMRC every 12 months	
(d)	The VAT payment has to be made in 12 equal monthly instalments	

Which **one** of these options is correct?

3.10   The flat rate scheme requires that:

(a)	VAT is charged at a single fixed rate on both input VAT and output VAT	
(b)	The amount due to HMRC is charged at a fixed rate on the total supplies for each VAT period	
(c)	Output VAT is charged at a fixed rate and input VAT is charged at a lower rate	
(d)	VAT invoices must show the fixed rate charged by HMRC for the supplies made	

Which **one** of these options is correct?

3.11   The cash accounting scheme:

(a)	Is normally operated in conjunction with the flat rate scheme	
(b)	Allows for VAT to be paid by monthly instalments	
(c)	Allows businesses to account for VAT on the basis of the date of payments received	
(d)	Requires a supplier to submit a VAT Return once every 12 months	

Which **one** of these options is correct?

3.12   Decide whether each of the following statements about imports and exports of goods and services is true or false:

		True	False
(a)	Postponed accounting should be used for the export of goods		
(b)	Reverse charge applies to the import of services		
(c)	The export of services by a UK based business to a business located overseas is outside the scope of UK VAT		

3.13   State which of the three VAT special schemes each of the statements set out below relates to. Choose out of:

– annual accounting scheme

– cash accounting scheme

– flat rate scheme

Write annual, cash or flat in the boxes on the right for each option.

(a)	This scheme will automatically provide for relief on any bad debt	
(b)	A supplier submits a VAT Return once every twelve months	
(c)	Payment is charged at a percentage rate related to the type of business	
(d)	Payment can be made in nine equal monthly instalments	
(e)	This scheme may be operated with the annual accounting scheme	
(f)	The VAT Return is due two months after the VAT period	
(g)	This scheme accounts for output VAT on the date payment is received	
(h)	This scheme does not have to record every single VAT transaction	

3.14   A bookkeeper runs a business from their home. Their turnover is £85,200 excluding VAT and their costs of goods are £1,980 including VAT.

If the bookkeeper has registered for the flat rate scheme, what rate of VAT must they use?

(a)	5%	
(b)	14.5%	
(c)	16.5%	
(d)	20%	

Which **one** of these options is correct?

3.15   Jackie has bought an asset for £5,100, including standard rate VAT. She will use it 65% of the time for business use and the remainder for personal use. How much input VAT can Jackie reclaim on the asset?

(a)	£297.50	
(b)	£552.50	
(c)	£663.00	
(d)	£850.00	

Which **one** of these options is correct?

4 The VAT Return, errors, and penalties

this chapter covers...

- the records a business needs to keep for recording transactions involving VAT

- the accounting records involving VAT which are needed to provide the figures for the VAT Return

- how the VAT Control Account is set out and what is included

- how to adjust when too much input VAT has been claimed back or too little output tax has been paid to HMRC in error on a previous VAT Return

- how to adjust for the VAT content of any bad debts incurred by the business – ie amounts which include output VAT that have been billed to credit customers, but are never likely to be paid

The chapter goes on to explain:

- how the appropriate figures are entered onto the VAT Return and how it is submitted to HMRC including the requirements of Making Tax Digital

- the need for reconciling the VAT Return to the underlying accounting records and reasons why they may not reconcile

- penalties that HMRC can impose for late submission of VAT Returns and late payment of VAT due

- HMRC's right to charge interest on VAT that is due

- when HMRC can assess how much VAT it is owed

VAT RECORDS

VAT and VAT records

The accounting system of a VAT-registered business should record:

- input tax on purchases and expenses
- output tax on sales

Most businesses now use accounting software which is able to generate a VAT Return. Despite there being a wide variety of systems available, the basic principles will remain the same: data has to be collected periodically (normally quarterly) so that input tax and output tax can be included in the VAT Return and the amount owed to/by HMRC can be calculated.

The basic records that a business must maintain that relate specifically to VAT include:

- **copies of sales invoices** (numerical/date order) – these are the tax invoices which set out the output tax charged (if it is charged)
- **purchase invoices** (with a consecutive reference number) – these are the tax invoices showing the input tax that the business can normally reclaim
- **credit notes and debit notes received** relating to adjustments made to sales and purchase invoices
- **cash and petty cash transaction receipts** eg petty cash vouchers
- documentation relating to **goods exported**
- information about **deposits, advance payments, and delayed payments**
- a **VAT control account** – also known as a VAT Account – which records all items of input and output tax and provides data for the VAT Return

other business records

Additional business records involving VAT that should be kept by the business include:

- bank statements, paying-in slips, and cheque book stubs
- purchase orders and delivery notes
- cash books and petty cash books
- purchases and sales daybooks
- ledger accounts
- payroll records
- computer printouts and reports
- annual accounts

We will now look in more detail at the records needed for sales (output tax) and purchases and expenses (input tax). For the purposes of your studies we will look at a business that buys and sells on credit and uses a computerised accounting system. You should always bear in mind that there are also some businesses that trade on cash terms, receiving payments immediately.

records for output tax (sales)

Records for output tax include:

sales daybook

This lists sales made on credit and is compiled from sales invoices issued by the business. It normally has an analysis column for VAT which is totalled and used in the output VAT calculation.

sales returns daybook

Any credit given (eg for returned goods, adjustments for overcharges or for prompt payment discount taken by a customer) may involve VAT and deduction should be made from output tax. The sales returns daybook will have a VAT analysis column, and will be compiled from credit notes and debit notes issued.

cash book – receipts side

This includes a VAT analysis column, and records details of other receipts **not on credit** which involve output tax, eg cash sales. The VAT included in receipts from credit customers should not normally be analysed, as this has already been dealt with in the sales daybook when the invoice was issued. However, if the business operates the cash accounting scheme for VAT, the VAT on receipts from credit customers will need to be identified and posted from the cash book.

records for input tax (purchases and expenses)

Records for input tax include:

purchases daybook

This lists all purchases made on credit and analyses VAT for inclusion in the input VAT total.

purchases returns daybook

Any credit received (eg for returned goods, adjustments for overcharges) may involve VAT which should be deducted from input tax. The purchases returns daybook will have a VAT analysis column, and will be compiled from credit notes and debit notes.

cash book – payments side

This lists expenses paid by the business; VAT for anything bought on **non-credit items** should be taken from the cash book analysis column. VAT on payments for credit purchases should normally be ignored as the amounts paid include VAT that has already been dealt with in the purchases daybook when the invoice was received. However, if the business operates the cash accounting scheme for VAT, the VAT on payments to credit suppliers will need to be identified and posted from the cash book.

A business may also use a **petty cash book** with a VAT column to list small expenses. This VAT will need to be accounted for in the VAT calculations.

It is important to ensure that the figures that are included in the VAT Return are accurate and valid and have come from the appropriate daybook or journal. Most businesses must now use computerised accounting software to record their accounting transactions. These will automatically post the VAT on each transaction to the appropriate ledger and to the VAT account. The system will normally automatically generate the VAT Return at the end of the VAT period which is submitted automatically to HMRC. This process is covered in more detail in the Making Tax Digital section later in this chapter. It is important to ensure that the VAT Return has been correctly generated and agrees with, or reconciles to, the underlying records.

VAT CONTROL ACCOUNT

The central record for any VAT-registered business's bookkeeping system is the **VAT Control account**, or VAT account.

The balance of the VAT account represents the amount owing to (or due from) HMRC.

The example of a VAT Control Account on the next page shows entries for a business that normally has a surplus of output tax over input tax, ie the business pays VAT to HMRC. The second example show a completed account, with sample figures and explanatory notes.

The VAT control account is not a double-entry account in the strict sense; for example, items such as credit notes are deducted on each side rather than being entered on the opposite side. In practice the VAT control account will be maintained by the computerised accounting system and the figures for the VAT Return will be automatically generated, with some systems also producing a draft VAT Return.

Study the VAT account on the next page and read the notes on pages 79-80.

VAT Control Account – summary of entries

VAT deductible (input tax)	VAT payable (output tax)
Purchases Daybook VAT monthly totals, *less* any credit notes received/debit notes issued	Sales Daybook VAT monthly totals, *less* any credit notes issued/debit notes received
Cash Book – items not in Purchases Daybook	Cash Book – items not in Sales Daybook
Petty Cash Book – VAT on small expenses	VAT element of the fuel scale charge
Correction of error(s) from previous returns (within the threshold – see later in the chapter)	Correction of error(s) from previous returns (within the threshold – see later in the chapter)
Postponed VAT on imports	Postponed VAT on imports
Reverse charge VAT on import of services	Reverse charge VAT on import of services
Bad debt relief	
= TOTAL TAX DEDUCTIBLE	= TOTAL TAX PAYABLE
	less TOTAL TAX DEDUCTIBLE
	equals TAX PAYABLE ON VAT RETURN

VAT Control Account

VAT deductible: input tax			VAT payable: output tax		
		£			£
Purchases Daybook £10,500.00 *less* credit notes £175.00		10,325.00	Sales Daybook £18,110.50 *less* credit notes £275.00		17,835.50
Cash Book		750.00	Cash Book		960.50
Petty Cash Book		15.95			
Postponed VAT on imports		473.65	Postponed VAT on imports		473.65
Bad Debt relief		675.00	Correction of error		175.69
TOTAL INPUT TAX		12,239.60	TOTAL OUTPUT TAX		19,445.34
			less TOTAL INPUT TAX		12,239.60
			equals VAT DUE		7,205.74

input tax

This is the debit side of the VAT control account.

Purchases Daybook

£10,500.00 is the total of the input VAT in the VAT analysis columns in the Purchases Daybook.

£175 is the total VAT in the Purchases Returns Daybook.

Cash Book

£750 is the total VAT in the Cash Book (payments side).

Petty Cash Book

£15.95 is from the total VAT in the Petty Cash Book.

Postponed VAT on imports

£473.65 is the total VAT reclaimed in this period on imports accounted for through postponed VAT accounting.

Bad (irrecoverable) debt relief

Bad debt relief is covered later in this chapter.

output tax

This is the credit side of the VAT control account.

Sales Daybook

£18,110.50 is the total of the output VAT in the VAT analysis columns in the Sales Daybook.

£275 is the total VAT in the Sales Returns Daybook.

There may also be VAT on credit notes for prompt payment discount.

Cash Book

£960.50 is the total VAT in the Cash Book (receipts side).

Postponed VAT on imports

£473.65 is the total VAT due in this period on imports accounted for through postponed VAT accounting (note this is the same figure as is included in the debit side).

Correction of errors

This could be on the debit or credit side of the VAT account, depending on the error.

In this case the business owes HMRC £175.69 relating to an error on a previous VAT Return.

If the net error resulted in HMRC owing the business, the correction would be on the debit (input) side of the VAT Account.

Correction of errors is explained in more detail on the next page.

VAT due calculation

VAT due is calculated by deducting the total of the input VAT side from the total of the output VAT side:

£19,445.34 minus £12,239.60 equals £7,205.74

If the total input VAT on the debit side is greater than the total output VAT on the credit side, the business will reclaim VAT from HMRC. Therefore, the appropriate calculation will be shown in the VAT account on the left-hand side. This will happen for a business that sells zero-rated goods as VAT will be charged at 0% (ie no output VAT to account for) but it will be able to reclaim all allowable input VAT on purchases and expenses.

treatment of VAT paid and reclaimed

VAT actually paid or reclaimed **for the previous VAT period is not included in the VAT account**.

At the beginning of each VAT period the VAT account will have an opening balance which is either:

- VAT owed to HMRC – a credit balance brought forward, or

- VAT reclaimable from HMRC – a debit balance brought forward

When the VAT liability is paid (or received, if VAT is reclaimable) this will cancel out this opening balance and the net effect of the two entries in the VAT account will be nil.

NET ERRORS UP TO THE ERROR CORRECTION REPORTING THRESHOLD

You will have seen that the output VAT side of the VAT account on page 78 includes an error correction of £175.69. This correction is adding this amount of output VAT to what is due for the VAT period, ie increasing the output VAT figure in the VAT Return (Box 1). The business may not have recorded a sale in the previous VAT period and needs to account for the VAT .

Where a business discovers that it has made an error, or a number of errors, in a previous VAT Return, it may be able to adjust for this in the current VAT Return provided the error(s) is (are):

- below the **reporting threshold**

- not deliberate

- related to an accounting period that ended less than four years before

The error reporting threshold is the greater of:

- £10,000 or less and
- 1% of the total value of sales and all other outputs excluding VAT, up to a maximum of £50,000

Provided the net value of all errors is less than the error reporting threshold, the net errors can be corrected as an adjustment on the current VAT Return. This should be done by adding the amount due on sales and other output for tax due to HMRC (Box 1 on the VAT Return) or adding it to VAT reclaimed on purchases and other inputs for tax due to the business (Box 4 on the VAT Return).

Net error is the difference between the total errors in output tax and the total errors in input tax. In most cases there will only be one error, so this will be the net error. Typical errors include failure to charge output tax on chargeable sales, charging VAT at the wrong rate, or arithmetical errors in the accounts, although this is less likely where a computerised accounting system is used.

If the error is **over the reporting threshold** or is a **deliberate error**, the matter will need to be declared separately, in writing, to HMRC as a 'voluntary disclosure'.

THE VAT RETURN – ONLINE SUBMISSION

The figures from the VAT account will be transferred to the VAT Return. Where businesses use accounting software this will be done automatically.

Although you do not need to prepare a VAT Return for your assessment, it is important to know what it looks like, and what is include in each box.

A sample online VAT Return is shown on page 83.

The boxes are completed as follows:

1   **VAT due in the period on sales and other outputs**

This box includes the VAT due on all goods and services supplied in the period (output tax).

It should also include:

- VAT due on imports accounted for through postponed VAT accounting
- fuel scale charges
- reverse charge VAT
- supplies to employees
- goods taken for private use (if a member of staff or the owner takes goods out of the business for private use, VAT on these goods must be included in Box 1 even if the goods are not paid for)

This total should be adjusted for any credit notes issued by the business and any errors (below the correction threshold) on previous VAT Returns.

2 **VAT due in the period on acquisitions of goods made in Northern Ireland from EU member states***

3 **Total VAT due**

This is the total of boxes 1 and 2, and is calculated automatically when figures are input in Box 1 and 2.

4 **VAT reclaimed in the period on purchases and other inputs**

This box includes deductible VAT on business purchases (input tax).

This box will also include VAT:

- VAT due on imports accounted for through postponed VAT accounting

- reverse charge VAT

- on acquisitions of goods made in Northern Ireland from EU member states (the same amount as included in Box 2)*

- relating to bad debt relief

This total should be adjusted for any credit notes issued to the business and any errors (below the correction threshold) on previous VAT Returns.

5 **Net VAT to pay to, or reclaim from, HMRC**

This is the difference between the figures in boxes 3 and 4. If the Box 3 figure is greater than the Box 4 figure, this is the amount due to HMRC. If the Box 4 figure is greater than the Box 3 figure, this is the amount reclaimed from HMRC.

6 **Total value of sales and all other outputs excluding any VAT**

This box includes the total value of sales and other outputs excluding any VAT.

This will include exempt, standard, and zero-rated supplies and supplies to EU and non-EU states. It will also include the net part of any fuel scale charges

This total should be adjusted for any credit notes issued by the business.

7 **The total value of purchases and all other inputs excluding any VAT**

This box includes the net value of purchases and expenses excluding VAT.

This includes standard, zero and exempt supplies, imports, and acquisitions of goods brought into Northern Ireland from EU member states and reverse charge transactions.*

This total should be adjusted for any credit notes issued by the business.

8 **The total of supplies of goods and related services, excluding VAT, from Northern Ireland to EU member states***

9 **The total value of all acquisitions of goods and related services, excluding VAT, from EU member states to Northern Ireland***

* Note: the rules relating to Northern Ireland are not assessed in this unit.

VAT Return
01 Jan 24 to 31 Mar 24

VAT due on sales and other outputs	**1**
VAT due on intra-community acquisitions of goods made in Northern Ireland from EU Member States	**2**
Total VAT due (the sum of boxes 1 and 2)	**3**
VAT reclaimed on purchases and other inputs (including acquisitions from the EU)	**4**
Net VAT to be paid to Customs by you (difference between boxes 3 and 4)	**5**
Total value of sales and all other outputs excluding any VAT	**6**
Total value of purchases and all other inputs excluding any VAT	**7**
Total value of intra-community dispatches of goods and related costs, excluding any VAT, from Northern Ireland to EU Member States	**8**
Total value of intra-community acquisitions of goods and related costs, excluding any VAT, made in Northern Ireland from EU Member States	**9**

BAD DEBT RELIEF

We saw earlier in the chapter that a business can include bad debt relief in Box 4 of its VAT Return. We will now look at this in more detail.

A **bad debt** is an amount owing which a supplier writes off in its accounts because the debt is unlikely ever to be paid off – the buyer may have 'gone bust' for example.

Bad debt relief is the VAT scheme in which HMRC allows a business to claim back VAT which it has charged to a customer on a credit sale and already paid over to HMRC, and which it now has no chance of recovering. The conditions for bad debt relief are that:

- bad debt relief is available for debts which are more than six months overdue and less than four years and six months overdue

- the debt must also have been written off in the business's VAT account and transferred to a separate bad debt account

- the debt must not have been sold or handed to a factoring company

- the business did not charge more than the normal selling price for the items

If the business satisfies all the criteria for claiming bad debt relief, the amount of VAT being claimed for the bad debt should be added to Box 4 on the VAT Return.

Note that bad debt relief cannot be reclaimed when the cash accounting scheme is used as the VAT is not paid to HMRC until after the customer has paid the business.

Case Study

LAURIE LEE

Laurence Lee is VAT-registered who submits quarterly VAT Returns on 31 January, 30 April, 31 July, and 31 October. He has written off an invoice for £867 including standard rate VAT. The invoice was originally due for payment on 12 February 2024.

What is the earliest VAT quarter that Laurence can claim bad debt relief on this invoice, and how much can he claim?

solution

Laurence has already written off the bad debt so he can claim bad debt relief once it is six months overdue, ie from 12 August 2024. This means he can claim it in the quarter ending 31 October 2024.

The VAT element of this invoice that can be claimed as bad debt relief is:

£867 x 1/6 = £144.50

MAKING TAX DIGITAL FOR VAT

Making Tax Digital (MTD) is HMRC's initiative to encourage businesses to keep their accounts in a digital format. Its aim is to help make administration of tax easier and more efficient for businesses. VAT was the first tax for which MTD has been introduced.

A business that is required to comply with MTD must use **compatible accounting software** that is capable of:

- keeping and maintaining its accounting records

- preparing its VAT Returns

- communicating with HMRC digitally via HMRC's Application Programming Interface Platform (API) including submitting its VAT Return

  A business can check that its software is authorised and compatible on the HMRC website at https://www.gov.uk/guidance/find-software-thats-compatible-with-making-tax-digital-for-vat.

If a business is required to register for MTD because its taxable turnover is above the registration threshold, it must continue to keep digital records and submit its returns digitally even if its turnover later falls below the VAT threshold. However, if the business deregisters from VAT, or meets other exemption criteria, it is no longer required to keep digital records.

It is important to remember that MTD for VAT is not just about digitally filing VAT Returns. It also requires businesses to keep and preserve records digitally.

electronic submission of VAT Return to HMRC

The deadline for filing a VAT Return is **one month and seven days** after the end of the VAT period. (This does not apply if the business uses the Annual Accounting Scheme.)

So a business that uses the standard quarterly VAT scheme that has a quarter end of 30 April must submit its VAT Return by 7 June.

electronic payments to HMRC

Once the VAT Return has been submitted, any VAT due to HMRC must be paid electronically. HMRC recommends that this is done by direct debit. However, businesses can use other electronic payment methods including BACS.

If the business pays by direct debit, HMRC automatically collects payment from the business's bank account **three bank working days** after the VAT Return submission date.

Using the example above of a business that submits its quarterly VAT Return on 7 June for the quarter ended 30 April, HMRC will collect payment on 10 June (assuming that these three days do not fall on a weekend).

If the business fails to pay cleared funds into HMRC's bank account by the payment deadline or fails to have sufficient funds in its account to meet the direct debit, it may be penalised. This is covered in more detail later in this chapter.

electronic repayment by HMRC

In the same way that there are rules governing the timing and method of payment for VAT due to HMRC, there are also obligations imposed on HMRC if the net VAT in Box 5 of the VAT Return is a repayment due to the business. Where this is the case HMRC is obliged to schedule electronic repayment into the business's bank account. This will normally be within 10 working days but may take up to 21 days if HMRC has a query. Certain circumstances may mean that a repayment of VAT is not made automatically, for example if there is an outstanding amount owed to HMRC by the business.

DIFFERENCES BETWEEN THE VAT ACCOUNT AND THE ACCOUNTING RECORDS

If accounting records have been kept correctly, the balance on the VAT control account, ie VAT due to HMRC, should always agree with the VAT Return. Before submitting its VAT Return, a VAT-registered business must ensure that it agrees with the underlying accounting records.

If the VAT Return does not reconcile with the accounting records, this must be investigated. There are a number of reasons why this could happen including mis-posting to the VAT Control account and errors or omissions on the VAT Return.

why the VAT Return might not reconcile with the accounting records

We have already said that it is important to ensure that the VAT Return agrees with the underlying accounting records, but why might this not be the case?

We will now look at some possible reason for the VAT records and the VAT Return not reconciling.

data has been transferred incorrectly to the computerised accounting system

When a business moves from using a manual accounting scheme to using accounting software there is always the risk that the information may be transferred incorrectly. It is important to carefully check each figure that is entered in the software to ensure that it is accurate. Any suspense account balances that occur should be investigated and resolved before the system is used and a VAT Return is produced.

accounting software has been set up incorrectly

When a business uses accounting software it is important to ensure that the software is set up for the correct VAT scheme. Whilst most businesses operate the normal VAT scheme and submit quarterly returns, as we saw in the previous chapter some will operate the annual accounting scheme, flat rate accounting scheme, or the cash accounting scheme.

If the accounting software generates the VAT Return from the accounting entries, then it must be set up for the correct VAT scheme.

For example, if a business that uses the flat rate scheme has been wrongly set up for normal quarterly VAT accounting, the system will calculate the wrong amount owed to HMRC.

A similar issue would arise if a business was set up in the accounting software as operating the cash accounting scheme for VAT when it actually uses the normal VAT scheme. Under the cash accounting scheme the business will only account for input and output VAT when it actually receives or makes a payment, whereas under the normal VAT scheme, VAT is accounted for on credit invoices.

The effect of these two setup errors is illustrated in the two Case Studies that follow.

JOSIE JO LTD

Josie runs her own VAT-registered photography business, Josie Jo Ltd. She has been registered on the flat rate scheme for VAT for several years and has always used a spreadsheet for her accounts. Due to the introduction of Making Tax Digital Josie has moved to a new accounting software package but is not confident that she has set it up correctly.

As a photography business, Josie Joe Ltd's flat rate percentage is 11% and in the last quarter Josie paid HMRC £4,127.50.

Josie's total sales for the current quarter including standard rate VAT are £39,250. And she is expecting to pay HMRC £4,317.50.

Josie has just run the draft VAT Return for the current VAT quarter using her new accounting software and is concerned that the amount of VAT she has to pay HMRC is showing as £4,755.

Josie's purchases for the quarter were £10,720 including standard rate VAT.

Josie needs to work out why there is a difference between what she expected to pay and what her new software says she should pay.

solution

As Josie has been using the flat rate scheme for several years, the amount that she pays HMRC each quarter is calculated as her sales for the quarter multiplied by her flat rate percentage. For this quarter she has correctly calculated this as £4,317.50, ie £39,250 x 11%.

If Josie has set up her accounting software for normal VAT accounting, it will calculate the amount due to HMRC as follows:

Output VAT	£39,250 x 20/120	= £6,541.66
Input VAT	£10,720 x 20/120	= £1,786.66
VAT payable to HMRC		£4,755.00

It appears that Josie has set up her accounting software incorrectly as if she was operating normal VAT accounting. Before submitting her VAT Return online, Josie should contact the software provider to explain the issue. They should then be able to give her assistance in setting up her software correctly.

Case Study

LIBBY LIB LTD

Libby Lib Ltd has recently moved from a manual accounting system to using accounting software. The business has been considering moving from normal VAT accounting to cash accounting but has not yet decided to do this.

Raymond, the finance assistant, who set up the new accounting software, has produced the draft VAT Return for the quarter ended 31 August 2023.

Extract from the draft VAT Return for the quarter to 31 August 2023:

	£
Box 1	19,450.00
Box 4	–4,420.00
Box 5	15,030.00
Box 6	97,250
Box 7	22,100

The owner, Libby Bee, has asked him to reconcile the VAT Return to the VAT liability in the trial balance before the VAT Return is submitted. Raymond has found that the figures do not agree. The VAT liability in the trial balance is £26,205.00 and Raymond has extracted the figures below from the VAT account in the nominal ledger.

		£
1 June 2023	Brought forward	9,728.50
10 July 2023	Paid to HMRC	–9,728.50
31 August 2023	Output VAT	31,835.00
31 August 2023	Input VAT	5,630.00
31 August 2023	Carried forward	26,205.00

He has also extracted the closing trade receivables figure of £74,310 (including standard rate VAT) and the closing trade payables figure of £7,260 (including standard rate VAT).

solution

Raymond realises that he has set the accounting software up incorrectly for cash accounting and decides to reconcile the figure in the draft VAT Return with the trial balance to confirm this.

He calculates the difference between the input and output VAT in the nominal ledger and in the draft VAT Return, and compares it to the VAT on the amounts due from and to trade receivables and payables at the end of the quarter which should be included in the VAT Return for the quarter.

Output tax:	£31,835 – £19,450	= £12,385
Equal to the VAT on the closing trade receivables ie £74,310 x 1/6		= £12,385
Input tax:	£5,630 – £4,420	= £1,210
Equal to the VAT on the closing trade payables ie £7,260 x 1/6		= £1,210

Raymond then reconciles the two figures by adding the additional output tax and subtracting the additional input tax that should be accounted for in the VAT Return.

Reconciliation	
	£
VAT liability per the draft VAT Return	15,030.00
Output VAT on closing trade receivables	12,385.00
Input VAT on closing trade payables	-1,210.00
VAT liability per the trial balance	26,205.00

He then makes the necessary changes to the accounting software and asks Libby to review them. Finally he produces the correct VAT Return below including an explanation of the reconciliation for Libby.

Revised extract from the VAT Return for the quarter to 31 August 2023:

	£	£
	(explanation)	
Box 1	19,450.00 + 12,385.00	31,835.00
Box 4	4,420.00 + 1,210.00	–5,630.00
Box 5		26,205.00
Box 6	97,250 + (74,310 x 100/120)	159,175
Box 7	22,100 + (7,260 x 100/120)	28,150

LATE SUBMISSION PENALTIES

We know that a VAT-registered business must submit its VAT Return by the HMRC deadline – one month and seven days after the end of the VAT period for quarterly or monthly VAT Returns, and two months after the end of the VAT period for a business that submits annual VAT Returns.

late submission penalties

If a business submits its VAT Return late it will be subject to late submission penalties which work on a points-based system.

The business will receive a penalty point for each return that is submitted late until it reaches the penalty point threshold at which point it will have to pay a £200 penalty. It will then receive a further £200 penalty for every subsequent late submission while it is at the points threshold.

A newly registered business will not be penalised if its first Return is late.

penalty point thresholds

The penalty point threshold for a business will depend on its accounting period. The threshold is the maximum points a business can receive.

Submission frequently	Penalty point threshold
Annually	2 points
Quarterly	4 points
Monthly*	5 points

* for information only – the assessment for this unit does not test penalties for businesses with monthly VAT Returns.

The following example illustrates how late submission penalties work:

Case Study

DEXUDO LTD

Dexudo Ltd, a VAT-registered business, submits its VAT Returns on a quarterly basis. The current VAT quarter ended on 30 April. It has already submitted three previous VAT Returns late, so has three penalty points. It submits its VAT Return on 14 June, which is late as it was due on 7 June. This results in a fourth penalty point. Because it has reached the penalty point threshold, Dexudo Ltd receives a £200 penalty.

Dexudo Ltd submits its next return for the quarter ended 31 July, on 4 September. Because this return has been submitted on time, the business stays at the threshold of four penalty points, but does not get a further £200 penalty.

The business then submits its VAT Return for the quarter ended 31 October on 9 December. Again, this is late. As Dextudo Ltd is still at the penalty point threshold of four points, it will receive another £200 penalty.

removal of penalty points – threshold not reached

If a business has not reached the late submission penalty threshold, individual penalty points will expire automatically, two years (24 months) from the first day of the month after the month when the late submission occurred. This can be illustrated by the following example.

Terrell Ltd has received the following penalty points:

Late submission of VAT Return for the quarter ended 31 March 2023 – one penalty point

Late submission of VAT Return for the quarter ended 30 June 2023 – one penalty point

In this situation the submission for the quarter ended 31 March 2023 should have been on 7 May 2023, so the penalty point for late submission will automatically expire on 1 June 2025, ie 24 months after 1 June 2023. The point for the quarter ended 30 June 2023 will expire on 1 September 2025.

removal of penalty points – threshold reached

Once a business has reached the late submission penalty threshold, ie it has the maximum points, the points can only be reset to zero if it meets the following two conditions:

Condition A – complete a period of compliance

Condition B – submit all outstanding returns for the previous 24 months (regardless of whether they were on time or not).

period of compliance (condition A)

A period of compliance is a period when a business submits all its returns on time. The earliest date a business can start a period of compliance is the first day of the month following the day after the missed deadline. For example, for a missed submission date of 7 August the earliest start of a period of compliance would be 1 September. However, if the business submits annual VAT Returns and the missed submission date is 30 June, the period of compliance would start on 1 August.

The length of the period of compliance depends how frequently a business submits its VAT Returns.

Submission frequently	Period of compliance
Annually	24 months
Quarterly	12 months
Monthly*	6 months

* for information only – the assessment for this unit does not test penalties for businesses with monthly VAT Returns.

This means that a business that makes quarterly VAT Returns will need to submit four VAT Returns on time during a period of compliance, and a business that submits annual VAT Returns will need to submit two.

submit all outstanding returns (condition B)

The second condition for removing late payment penalty points is that outstanding VAT Returns for the previous 24 months must have been submitted, even if they were not on time. It's worth noting that the 24 months will include the period of compliance.

The following example illustrates the removal of penalty points.

Note: this example refers to dates in 2024 as the late submission penalties were only introduced in 2023.

Case Study

FLORIS

Floris submits quarterly VAT Returns, so has a late submission penalty threshold of four points. By 7 September 2024, it has reached the late submission penalty threshold because it did not submit its VAT Returns on the following due dates:

7 June 2023 (VAT Return for the quarter ended 30 April 2023)

7 December 2023 (VAT Return for the quarter ended 31 October 2023)

7 March 2024 (VAT Return for the quarter ended 31 January 2024)

7 September 2024 (VAT Return for the quarter ended 31 July 2024)

How does Floris ensure that its penalty points are removed?

solution

meet condition A

To meet condition A, Floris must submit all VAT returns on time for 12 months (the period of compliance for quarterly VAT Returns). As 7 September 2024 was the date of the most recent missed deadline, the 12-month period of compliance starts on 1 October 2024 at the earliest and ends 12 months later, on 30 September 2025. This means that Floris must submit all four VAT Returns that are due between 1 October 2024 and 31 August 2025, on time.

meet condition B

To meet condition B, Floris must have submitted all outstanding VAT Returns due in the previous 24 months.

If Floris has met condition A, this means it has submitted the VAT Returns due between 1 October 2024 and 31 August 2025.

The penalty points detailed earlier relate to submissions due in March 2024 and September 2024. When Floris has submitted these two returns it will have submitted all outstanding VAT Returns due in the previous 24 months and met condition B.

Floris's penalty points will be set to zero on the date that both conditions are met.

LATE PAYMENT PENALTIES

Businesses that owe VAT to HMRC must pay the amount due by the payment deadline. For quarterly VAT accounting where a business pays by direct debit, this is one month and seven days after the end of the VAT quarter, plus three working days. If the business does not pay by direct debit, the deadline is one month and seven days after the end of the VAT quarter. If the payment is late there is a series of late payment penalties that will be imposed on the business. These late payment penalties can apply to payments due:

- on a VAT Return

- following an amendment to a return or correction

- from a VAT assessment HMRC issued when a business did not submit its return

- from a VAT assessment HMRC issued for another reason

Penalties do not apply to:

- VAT payments on account

- instalments for the VAT Annual Accounting Scheme

first and second late payment penalties

A business will get a first late payment penalty if its payment is 16 or more days overdue – this means that there is no late penalty for the first 15 days that the amount is overdue if it is a business's first late payment penalty.

Once the payment becomes 31 or more days overdue, the first late payment penalty increases, and the business gets a second late payment penalty.

	First late payment penalty	**Second late payment penalty**
Payment up to 15 days overdue	None	None
Payment between 16 and 30 days overdue	2% on the VAT outstanding at day 15	None
Payment 31 days, or more overdue	2% on the VAT outstanding at day 15 plus 2% on the VAT outstanding at day 30	A daily rate based on 4% per annum, charged every day from day 31, until paid in full

The application of these penalties is best explained using an example.

RANSTO LTD

Ransto Ltd is a VAT-registered business that submits its VAT Returns quarterly. It has submitted its May 2023 VAT Return by the deadline of 7 July 2023. However, Ransto Ltd has cancelled its direct debit to HMRC, so HMRC does not receive the £12,000 VAT Ransto Ltd owes on time.

HMRC sends Ransto Ltd a late payment reminder letter asking it to pay in full to avoid penalties. The penalties that Ransto Ltd pays (or does not pay) will depend on how quickly it pays the amount outstanding.

solution

payment up to 15 days overdue

If Ransto Ltd pays in full by the end of day 15, it will not get a late payment penalty.

payment is between 16 and 30 days overdue

If Ransto Ltd makes full payment on 27 July 2023, this is between 16 and 30 days after the VAT is due. The first late payment penalty is calculated at 2% of the VAT that was outstanding at the end of the day 15. HMRC charges a first late payment penalty of:

2% of £12,000 = £240

payment is 31 days or more overdue

If Ransto Ltd pays the VAT that it owes on 24 August 2023, this is 48 days after the date it was due.

The **first late payment penalty** that HMRC charges Ransto Ltd is calculated as:

2% of the amount outstanding at day 15, ie 2% of £12,000	= £240
2% of the amount outstanding at day 30, ie 2% of £12,000	= £240
Total late payment penalty	= £480

Because the amount is now 31 or more days overdue, HMRC also charges Ransto Ltd a **second late payment penalty**. This is calculated daily at a rate equivalent to 4% per annum on the £12,000 overdue.

The period of time from day 31 of the payment being overdue (7 August 2023) up to and including day 48 (24 August) when Ransto Ltd paid in full works out as 18 days, so the calculation is:

£12,000 x 4% x 18/365 = £23.67

This means that the total late payment penalty that Ransto Ltd is charged for paying 48 days late is £503.67, ie:

first late payment penalty	£480
second late payment penalty	£23.67

INTEREST CHARGED ON VAT

In addition to late payment penalties, HMRC charges late payment interest on overdue payments.

payments on which interest is charged

Interest will be charged on all late payments where VAT is due. This includes amounts overdue following:

- a VAT Return

- an amendment or correction of a VAT Return

- a VAT assessment made by HMRC (see next section)

- a missed VAT payment on account, ie under the annual accounting scheme

Interest will also be charged on all **penalties** if they are overdue including:

- late payment penalties for late payment of VAT

- late submission penalties for not submitting a return on time

Late payment interest is charged from the first day that the payment is overdue until the day it is paid in full. It is calculated at the Bank of England base rate plus 2.5%.

The following example illustrates late payment interest.

Case Study

JESTY LTD

Jesty Ltd is a VAT-registered business that submits and pays quarterly VAT Returns. Jesty Ltd's latest VAT quarter ends on 31 January 2024.

Jesty Ltd submitted the VAT Return on time on 7 March 2024 which was the deadline for submission. The VAT Retun showed that it owed HMRC £9,350 VAT. Jesty Ltd did not make the payment to HMRC until 19 March 2024, 12 days later than the due date.

The Bank of England base rate is currently 5% (if you need to do an interest calcuation in your assessment you will be given the base rate).

How much late payment interest will Jesty Ltd pay?

solution

The late payment interest will be charged at 7.5% (5% + 2.5%)

The late payment interest Jesty will be charged is calcuated as:

£9,350 x 7.5% x 12/365 days) = £23.05

claiming interest on VAT

A business may be able to claim interest if HMRC makes a mistake that means:

- the business pays too much VAT
- the business reclaims too little VAT
- a payment to the business from HMRC has been delayed

If HMRC owes repayment interest, this is calculated at the Bank of England base rate minus 1%, with a minimum rate of 0.5%. This is normally paid for the whole period from when the VAT was overpaid or reclaimed, until the date repayment by HMRC is authorised.

Normally HMRC will not repay interest if a business has paid too much VAT because of a mistake the business made.

ASSESSMENT OF VAT

In addition to the penalties already covered in this chapter, a business that fails to submit its VAT Return on time will be issued with a **VAT notice of assessment of tax**. This will show how much VAT HMRC thinks that the business owes.

If this assessment turns out to be too low, and the business does not tell HMRC that the assessment is incorrect within 30 days, HMRC can then charge a penalty that is 30% of the assessment amount.

If a business submits a paper VAT Return, and it has not been told by HMRC that it is exempt from submitting its return online or using Making Tax Digital compatible software, the business may be charged a £400 penalty.

a final point

Failure to pay VAT due or penalties that are imposed is a **criminal offence** and can result in prosecution.

Chapter Summary

■ It is important that a business maintains accurate and comprehensive accounting records, and keeps the records for at least six years. They may be needed for inspection by HMRC.

■ VAT records that must be kept include:

– copies of sales invoices

– originals of purchase invoices

– credit notes issued and received

– cash and petty cash transactions receipts

– documents relating to exports

– information relating to deposits, advance payments and delayed payments

– VAT control account

– other associated records

■ Most VAT-registered businesses use computerised accounting software. The normal sources of accounting data for the completion of the VAT Return are:

– sales and purchases daybooks, and returns daybooks (for credit items)

– cash book and petty cash book (for non-credit items)

■ This data is compiled in a VAT control account.

■ Net VAT errors of £10,000 or less, or 1% of quarterly turnover, subject to a £50,000 maximum limit, can be corrected on a subsequent VAT Return. Errors over these limits should be advised as a 'written voluntary disclosure' to HMRC.

■ It is important that the VAT Return is reconciled with the accounting records to ensure that the figures are correct before the VAT Return is submitted.

■ The VAT account may also be used to make adjustments for errors on previous VAT Returns that are under the error reporting threshold and for Bad Debt Relief which will reimburse a business for output VAT charged on a debt which has been written off.

■ Making Tax Digital (MTD) for VAT requires the majority of VAT-registered businesses to use compatible accounting software that is capable of keeping and maintaining their accounting records, preparing their VAT Returns and communicating with HMRC digitally via HMRC's Application Programming Interface Platform.

■ Most VAT Returns must be submitted online one month and seven days after the end of the VAT period. HMRC will collect payment three working days later from businesses that pay by direct debit.

■ HMRC has a points-based penalty regime for late sumission of VAT Returns. The points threshold for a business will depend on how often it submits a VAT Return, quarterly or annually. Penalty points automatically expire after two years if the business has not reached the threshold. A business that has reached the threshold will have to comply with certain conditions to have the points removed.

■ HMRC imposes penatlies on a business that makes payments late. This will depend on how late the payment is, and whether it is a first or a second late payment penalty.

■ HMRC will charge a business interest on unpaid VAT if the business reports less VAT than is due, if an assessment is paid which is lower than the actual VAT due, or if the business informs HMRC that it owes VAT because of an error on a previous VAT Return. This interest is charged at the Bank of England base rate plus 2.5%.

■ A business can claim interest if it has paid too much VAT, but HMRC will normally only pay if it has made the mistake rather than the business.

■ A business that fails to submit its VAT Return on time will be issued with a VAT notice of assessment of tax showing how much VAT HMRC thinks the business owes.

VAT control account	a control account that collects all the accounting data needed for the VAT Return; it is not a double-entry account
net errors reporting threshold	net VAT errors of £10,000 or less, or 1% of quarterly turnover, subject to a £50,000 maximum limit, can be corrected on a subsequent VAT Return. Errors over these limits must be separately disclosed to HMRC
VAT Return	the VAT Return is submitted electronically by VAT-registered businesses at the end of each VAT period in order to calculate the amount of VAT due to HMRC or reclaimable from HMRC
bad debt relief	a scheme that allows a VAT-registered business to reclaim any output VAT paid over to HMRC on credit sale which has subsequently gone 'bad' (over six months after the due date)
Making Tax Digital	HMRC's requirement for VAT-registered businesses to keep digital records and submit VAT Returns using compatible software
late submission penalties	a penalty regime where HMRC can impose penalty points if a business submits its VAT Return late on one or more occasions
late payments penalties	a regime of penalties that can be imposed if payments to HMRC are late
Bank of England base rate	the rate of interest the Bank of England charges other banks and other lenders when they borrow money. It is used to calculate late payment interest charged by HMRC (Bank of England base rate plus 2.5%)
VAT notice of assessment	notice issued by HMRC when a business does not submit its VAT Return on time. It will state how much VAT HMRC thinks is owed

Activities

4.1   A business can use the following records as a source of information for **input VAT** to include in the VAT Control Account:

(a)	Sales daybook, cash book (payments side), petty cash book (payments)	
(b)	Purchases daybook, cash book (payments side), petty cash book (payments)	
(c)	Purchases daybook, cash book (receipts side), purchases returns daybook	
(d)	Sales daybook, cash book (payments side), purchases returns daybook	

Which **one** of these options is correct?

4.2   A business can use the following records as a source of information for **output VAT** to include in the VAT Account:

(a)	Sales daybook, cash book (receipts side), petty cash book (payments)	
(b)	Purchases daybook, cash book (payments side), purchases returns daybook	
(c)	Sales daybook, cash book (payments side), purchases returns daybook	
(d)	Sales daybook, cash book (receipts side), sales returns daybook	

Which **one** of these options is correct?

4.3   A business that has overclaimed input tax of £120 in error on the last VAT Return should:

(a)	Add it to the input tax side of the VAT Account as an error correction	
(b)	Deduct it from the Sales Daybook monthly VAT total in the VAT Account	
(c)	Deduct it from the input tax side of the VAT Account as an error correction	
(d)	Add it to the Bad Debt Relief figure in the VAT Account	

Which **one** of these options is correct?

4.4 Julienne has entered an invoice from a new supplier for £635.04, including standard rate VAT at 20%. The accounting software has calculated the VAT included in the invoice as £30.24. However, the invoice shows the VAT as £105.84. Which two of the following statements are correct?

(a)	The VAT on the invoice is incorrect and Julienne should request a correct invoice from the supplier	
(b)	The accounting software has incorrectly calculated the VAT on the invoice at reduced rate	
(c)	The accounting software has correctly calculated the VAT on the invoice at the standard rate	
(d)	Julienne needs to adjust the VAT rate for the supplier in the accounting software	

Which **two** of these options are correct?

4.5 A business has written off a customer account as a bad debt. The written-off amount included VAT of £48 which has been accounted for in a previous VAT Return. This amount should be:

(a)	Added to the Box 1 figure on the VAT Return	
(b)	Deducted from the Box 1 figure on the VAT Return	
(c)	Added to the Box 4 figure on the VAT Return	
(d)	Deducted from the Box 4 figure on the VAT Return	

Which **one** of these options is correct?

4.6 Aisha does not operate any of the special accounting schemes. Her VAT Quarters end on 31 March, 30 June, 30 September, and 31 December. On 15 October, she has written off an invoice for £4,680 including standard rate VAT. The invoice was originally due for payment on 3 June.

(a) How much bad debt relief can Aisha claim on this invoice?

£ [   ]

(b) The earliest point that Aisha can claim bad debt relief on this invoice is the VAT Period ending:

[   ]

(c) Aisha will claim the bad debt relief by adding the VAT calculated in (a) to the Box ___ figure on her VAT Return.

4.7 Jeanie submits VAT Returns quarterly and pays HMRC by direct debit. Her latest quarter end is 30 June. Decide whether the following statement is true or false.

'HMRC will collect payment from Jeanie's bank account on 7 August.'

4.8   James has identified an error that he made in the previous quarter's VAT Return. He has posted an invoice from a supplier for £3,240, including VAT at standard rate, twice in the accounting software.

(a)   How much will the adjustment need to be for this error in the current quarter's VAT Return?

£ [   ]

(b)   This adjustment will _____ on the VAT Return.

Select one of the following options to complete the sentence:

increase input tax; increase output tax; decrease input tax; decrease output tax

4.9   Burstein Ltd made sales in the previous quarter totalling £862,500. What is the reporting threshold for errors in the previous quarter's VAT for Burstein Ltd?

(a)	£8,625	
(b)	£10,000	
(c)	£43,125	
(d)	£50,000	

Which **one** of these options is correct?

4.10   Shona owns and runs a bathroom fitting business. She has taken two heated towel rails for her own use in her bathrooms at home. Each towel rail cost £510, including VAT at standard rate. How should Shona treat this in her next VAT Return?

(a)	Include £1,020 in Box 1 of her VAT Return	
(b)	Take £170 off the total in Box 4 of her VAT Return	
(c)	Include £170 in Box 1 of the VAT Return	
(d)	She does not need to do anything as it is her business	

Which **one** of these options is correct?

4.11 Rollway Ltd has changed accounting software that it uses to calculate VAT. Rollway Ltd operates the cash accounting scheme for VAT.

The accounts assistant has produced the draft VAT Return for the quarter ended 31 May 2023, and his manager has asked him to prepare a reconciliation to the trial balance before the final VAT Return is submitted.

The draft VAT Return for the quarter to 31 May 2021 contains the following figures:

	£
Box 1	12,917.00
Box 4	−7,091.00
Box 5	5,826.00
Box 6	64,585
Box 7	35,455

The VAT liability in the trial balance is £499.00 and the accounts assistant has extracted the figures below from the VAT account in the nominal ledger:

		£
1 March 2023	Brought forward	1,040.20
10 April 2023	Paid to HMRC	−1,040.20
31 May 2023	Output VAT	5,243.00
31 May 2023	Input VAT	4,744.00
31 May 2023	Carried forward	499.00

He has also extracted the closing trade receivables figure of £46,044 (including standard rate VAT) and the closing trade payables figure of £14,082 (including standard rate VAT).

(a) Identify which **one** of the following is the reason for the difference between the VAT liability figure in the trial balance and the figure on the draft VAT Return.

(a)	The accounting software has been incorrectly set up for normal accounting for VAT	
(b)	The accounting software has been incorrectly set up for cash accounting for VAT	
(c)	The accounting software has been correctly set up for normal accounting for VAT	

(b) Complete the reconciliation below between the figure in the draft VAT Return and the figure in the trial balance.

Reconciliation	
	£
VAT liability per the draft VAT Return	
VAT liability per the trial balance	499.00

4.12 In relation to Making Tax Digital for VAT, the abbreviation API stands for which of the following?

(a)	Advanced programming interface	
(b)	Application programming interface	
(c)	Approved programming interface	
(d)	Application programming intermediary	

Which **one** of these options is correct?

4.13 Moira, the financial accountant at Kelpex Ltd, has been unwell over the past few months. This has meant that the VAT Returns for the last two quarters have both been submitted late. Kelpex Ltd has never previously submitted a VAT Return late.

(a) How many late submission penalty points will Kelpex Ltd receive?

(a)	One	
(b)	Two	
(c)	Three	
(d)	Four	

Which **one** of these options is correct?

(b)   What is the late submission penalty point threshold for Kelpex Ltd?

(a)	Two points	
(b)	Three points	
(c)	Four points	
(d)	Ten points	

Which **one** of these options is correct?

(c)   Decide whether each of the following statement is true or false.

		True	False
(a)	Because Kelpex Ltd has reached the penalty point threshold it must complete a period of compliance before the points are removed		
(b)	Because Kelpex Ltd has not reached the penalty point threshold each point will expire two years (24 months) from the first day of the month after the month when the late submission occurred		
(c)	Kelpex Ltd will not incur any financial penalty as it has received late penalty points		

4.14   Jenisco Ltd is a VAT-registered business that submits its VAT Returns quarterly. It has submitted its June 2023 VAT Return on time. However, Jenisco Ltd has changed the authorisation requirements on its bank account which has meant that the VAT direct debit was cancelled and HMRC has been unable to collect the £16,500 due by direct debit.

HMRC sent Jenisco Ltd a late payment reminder letter, but the payment was not made until 28 September 2023.

(a)   By what date should the payment have been made?

(a)	30 June 2023	
(b)	7 July 2023	
(c)	31 July 2023	
(d)	7 August 2023	

Which **one** of these options is correct?

(b) Calculate the first late payment penalty for the quarter ended 30 June 2023.

£ _____

(c) Calculate the second late payment penalty for the quarter ended 30 June 2023. Show your answer to the nearest £.

£ _____

5   Principles of payroll

this chapter covers...

This chapter starts by explaining the responsibility of businesses and individuals who employ staff to register as employers and operate a payroll. It then goes on to identify the powers HMRC, the tax authority for payroll, has to require businesses to:

- register as an employer
- keep payroll records
- submit returns
- pay amounts due

The chapter looks at HMRC's rules about:

- what records should be kept
- what payroll software an employer must use to submit its online payroll information
- how payroll records should be retained, and for how long
- the data protection principles in relation to personal data held about employees.

The next section of the chapter then covers payroll calculations, differentiating between gross pay, taxable pay, and net pay, and explaining the statutory and non-statutory deductions that an employer must make from payroll. Statutory deductions include:

- Pay As You Earn (PAYE)
- National Insurance Contributions (NICs)

■ *student loans*

■ *pensions*

The chapter then looks at the content of the forms produced for payroll, and when they must be provided to employees. The forms covered are:

■ *payslip*

■ *P45*

■ *P60*

■ *P11D*

*The final part of the chapter covers reporting to HMRC, and the fact that payroll must be submitted in real time (**RTI**). It explains the content of full payment submissions (**FPS**) and the employer payment summary (**EPS**) reports submitted under RTI. It also identifies the time limits for submission, together with the consequences of late filing and late payment.*

INTRODUCTION TO PAYROLL

Any business or individual that employs staff must operate a payroll system. Employment in the UK is regulated by government legislation which is designed to protect workers. Employees should have a contract of employment that specifies the amount they will receive for the work that they do and when payment will be received.

The government department that is in charge of collection of taxes is HM Revenue & Customs (HMRC). There are strict rules and regulations that must be complied with to ensure that:

■ employees are paid the correct amount on or before the due date

■ deadlines are met for making payments to HMRC, pension providers, courts, and other external bodies

■ any changes to payroll information are dealt with promptly

We will look at these requirements later in this chapter, and at the consequences of failure to adhere to payroll legislation.

registering as an employer

A business or person is normally required to register as an employer with HMRC when it starts to employ staff (or starts to use subcontractors for construction work). An individual must also register as an employer even if they are only employing themselves, ie as the only director of a limited company, and are going to pay themselves.

An employer must **register before the first payday** but cannot register more than two months before it starts to pay its employees. It can take up to five working days for a business to receive its employee PAYE reference number.

A business that has an online tax account can use this to register as an employer. HMRC requires the following information to register:

■ Business Unique Tax Reference (UTR)

■ Business Name

■ Business address

■ Date first payment will be made to employees

■ Number of employees, including directors

■ Whether the business needs to register for CIS

■ Whether the business intends to provide expenses and benefits to employees

■ Contact email address

■ Sole trader name (if business is run by a sole trader) or if business is a limited company, directors' names

■ Sole trader or director(s)' National Insurance numbers

payroll software

HMRC requires employers to run their payrolls using computerised payroll software. This allows employers to transmit up-to-date information electronically to HMRC about who they employ and what they have paid these employees. This online process is called Real Time Information (RTI).

Depending on its size, a business can decide to do one of the following:

■ use a commercial payroll bureau to provide its payroll function. The employer will provide the bureau, often an accounting practice, with employee and pay information, and the bureau will use commercial software to process the payroll and liaise online with HMRC on behalf of the client

■ purchase payroll software from a software supplier that has been tested and is recognised by HMRC. These products can be found at www.gov.uk/payroll-software/paid-for-software

■ download free payroll software that has been tested and recognised by HMRC for businesses with fewer than 10 employees. This can be found at www.gov.uk/payroll-software/free-software

HMRC will not recommend payroll software, but will have tested the free, or paid-for, software to check that it can report Pay As You Earn (PAYE) information online and in real time (RTI).

Before selecting payroll software, it is important that an employer considers which features it needs. Some payroll software will not allow the user to produce payslips, record pension deductions, make pension payments, or pay different employees over different time periods, for example both weekly and monthly.

The government sets the tax rates and allowances, which will then be updated for each tax year. Currently, the tax year runs from 6th April to the following 5th April. A business should ensure that it updates its payroll software from 6 April or earlier if the software provider asks it to, as this will ensure that the software is using the latest rates and thresholds for Income Tax, National Insurance, and student loan repayments. Tax months run from 6th of one month to 5th of the next. The month 6th April to 5th May is referred to as month 1 of the tax year, 6th May to 5th June is month 2, and so on.

RECORD KEEPING FOR PAYROLL

HMRC has rules relating to the payroll records that an employer must keep and how these records must be kept.

required records to be kept

HMRC states that an employer must collect and keep records of:

- what it pays its employees and what deductions it makes
- reports it makes to HMRC
- payments it makes to HMRC
- details of employee leave and sickness absence
- tax code notices
- taxable expenses or benefits
- payroll giving scheme documents

These records must contain sufficient detail to show that the employer has reported accurately to HMRC, and must be kept for three years after the end of the tax year to which they relate. Many employers will keep payroll records for six years in line with the requirements for the retention of other tax and accounting records. Most payroll records will be stored electronically.

The penalty for failure to maintain payroll records is £3,000.

personal data about employees

Employers are permitted to keep the following data about their employees without their permission:

- name

- address
- date of birth
- sex
- education and qualifications
- work experience
- National Insurance (NI) number
- tax code
- emergency contact details
- employment history with the organisation
- employment terms and conditions (eg pay, hours of work, holidays, benefits, absence)
- any accidents connected with work
- any training taken
- any disciplinary action

However, employers need their employees' permission to keep certain types of 'sensitive' data, and must ensure that this data is kept more securely than other types of data. This sensitive data includes:

- race and ethnicity
- religion
- political membership or opinions
- trade union membership
- genetics
- biometrics, for example if their fingerprints are used for identification
- health and medical conditions
- sexual history or orientation

Employees have the right to be told:

- what records are kept about them and how they are used
- the confidentiality of the records
- how these records can help with their training and development at work

If an employee asks to find out what data is kept about them, their employer will have 30 days to provide a copy of the information.

data protection and payroll information

General Data Protection Regulation (GDPR) requires businesses to take steps to protect any personal information that they collect. The Data Protection Act 2018 controls how personal information is used by organisations, businesses, or the government.

Everyone responsible for using personal data, including data held about employees for payroll purposes, has to follow strict rules called **data protection principles**. These principles require organisations to ensure that information is:

- used fairly, lawfully, and transparently
- used for specified, explicit purposes
- used in a way that is adequate, relevant, and limited to only what is necessary
- accurate and, where necessary, kept up-to-date
- kept for no longer than is necessary
- handled in a way that ensures appropriate security, including protection against unlawful or unauthorised processing, access, loss, destruction, or damage

There are separate safeguards for personal data relating to criminal convictions and offences.

HMRC inspections and visits

HMRC is entitled to check the tax affairs of a business or an individual to ensure that they are paying the right amount of tax. As part of this HMRC can check PAYE records and returns if a business or individual employs people. HMRC will write to, or phone, the employer to explain what it wants to check. It will then arrange to visit the business or its accountant's office, or for a representative of the business to visit HMRC. Failure to comply with the visit, or to send HMRC the information it requires, may result in a penalty unless the employer has a reasonable excuse such as serious illness or bereavement.

Once HMRC has completed its check it will write to the employer to tell them the results of the check. If the business has paid too much it will receive a refund (and possibly some interest if this is the fault of HMRC). However, if the business has not paid enough, it will be asked to pay the additional amounts within 30 days with interest charged from the day the amount was due. HMRC may also charge a penalty depending on the reasons for the underpayment, whether the business told HMRC as soon as possible and how helpful the business has been during HMRC's check. We will look at the penalties for late payment later in the chapter.

PAYROLL CALCULATIONS

Before we look at any payroll calculation it is important to understand the difference between gross pay, taxable pay, and net pay.

gross pay

Gross pay is pay before deductions like tax and National Insurance. It can be expressed as an annual amount, for example £24,000 per annum, or pay per period such as £450 per week or £2,000 per month. It can also be expressed as an hourly rate such as £13 per hour, or may include a lump sum such as a bonus of £1,500. Some employees will be paid a higher hourly rate for any overtime they work, which must also be factored into any payroll calculations. Normally employees who are paid overtime will prepare a timesheet which shows how many hours they have worked. This will be authorised by a manager before the payroll administrator, or the payroll bureau, calculates how much the employee should be paid.

Case Study

situation

Brindles Ltd employs a number of staff members on different types of contracts, three of which are detailed below:

- Sally Davis, the Sales Manager, is paid £36,900 per annum and is paid on a monthly basis

- Justine Moreso, the receptionist, is paid £480 per week for a 40 hour week. She is paid at time and a half for any overtime she does, and is paid weekly

- Ari Kotler works in the production department and is paid £600 per week. He is expected to produce 600 units per week, and is paid a productivity bonus of £2 for every unit over 600 that he produces in a week.

In the first week of May, Justine worked 43 hours, and Ari produced 623 units.

Calculate the gross pay for each of the employees for the period detailed below.

solution

Employee	Gross pay calculation			Gross pay	Pay period
Sally Davis	£36,900 pa ÷ 12 months			£3,075	Month of May
Justine Moreso	Basic hourly rate = £480 ÷ 40 hours		= £12 per hour		First week of May
	Overtime rate = £12 per hour x 1.5		= £18 per hour		
	Basic pay		= £480		
	Overtime	= 3 hours x £18	= £54	£534	
Ari Kotler	Basic pay		= £600		First week of May
	Bonus	= 23 units x £2	= £46	£646	

other elements of gross pay

In addition to the gross pay for work done that we have looked at, some employees may also be entitled to additional or alternative amounts. These include:

- holiday pay

- sick pay

- maternity pay

- paternity pay

These amounts may be all that is paid to the employee, or they may be paid in addition to other amounts. Either way, they must be recorded, and they are all subject to tax and National Insurance if certain thresholds (levels) are exceeded.

taxable pay

Taxable pay is the gross pay of an employee minus any tax-free elements, and is the amount on which Income Tax is charged. The government encourages some types of voluntary deduction from an employee's pay by allowing the amounts to be deducted before Income Tax is charged. The amount of tax saved is **tax relief**.

Tax relief is given on donations to charity which HMRC refers to as **payroll giving**. For example, if an employee has gross pay of £1,625 per month, and £25 is deducted from this as a donation to charity, the employee's taxable pay reduces to £1,600 per month.

Employee contributions to a company pension scheme that are collected through payroll will also attract tax relief. For example, if our employee who earns £1,625 per month pays 8% of their salary (£130) into an employer pension scheme, this will reduce their taxable pay by a further £130 per month to £1,470 (£1,600 – £130).

net pay

Net pay is sometimes referred to as 'take-home pay' and is the total pay and allowances minus total deductions. We will now look at the deductions that a business is required to make from gross pay.

STATUTORY AND NON-STATUTORY DEDUCTIONS

Once an employee's gross pay has been calculated, it is subject to a variety of possible deductions which an employer is entitled to make with, or without, the employee's authorisation, depending on whether they are statutory (ie required by law) or non-statutory (ie voluntary deductions).

- **statutory deductions** – an employee does not have to give written authorisation for statutory deductions as they are required by law

- **non-statutory deductions** – an employee must agree in writing for these deductions to be made from their pay

statutory deductions

Businesses are required to make statutory deductions from gross pay for:

- pay as you earn (PAYE)

- National Insurance Contributions (NICs)

- student loans

- pensions

pay as you earn (PAYE)

PAYE is the system for calculating and applying deductions for **Income Tax** in the UK. Income Tax is a direct tax that is paid on taxable income over a certain threshold. The amount of tax that an employee pays on their earnings is determined by their **tax code**, which is usually made up of a number and a letter – for example, 1257L. The number element of the tax code, multiplied by 10, is the amount of 'free pay', or untaxed pay, that the employee is entitled to in one year. This is the employee's **personal allowance** for tax. Any pay over this amount, up to a 'higher rate' threshold, is taxed at the 'basic rate' percentage (currently 20%). If an employee's annual taxable income is more than the higher rate threshold, tax is calculated at the 'higher rate' percentage (currently 40%) on the amount above the threshold. There is also an 'additional rate' tax rate (currently 45%) for taxable annual income above the additional rate threshold.

The letter in the tax code shows how the number should be adjusted if the government makes general changes to tax allowances. For example, if the letter is 'L' (as in 1257L) the government may advise that at the start of a new tax year all existing tax codes ending 'L' should have 30 added to the number (so 1257L would become 1287L). This avoids HMRC having to send out millions of new tax code notifications for individual people.

If the number of a tax code changes during the tax year, it may be because the employee has either paid too much, or too little, tax in the past and is a way for HMRC to collect or refund tax by restating the amount of free pay the employee is entitled to for the tax year. The employer must only change the tax code of an employee when advised to do so by HMRC notification. If a notification is received, the new tax code must be applied from the next payday, or as instructed by HMRC.

A computerised payroll system will be able to recognise the tax code of each individual employee and apply this to their gross earnings to determine their taxable pay. However, it is important that the payroll information is correctly entered into the system to ensure that the correct amounts are deducted.

national insurance contributions (NIC)

National Insurance is a system of compulsory payments made by employees and employers to the government to fund state assistance in the form of benefits for people who are sick, unemployed, or retired. This includes state pensions for people who have reached retirement age, jobseeker's allowance, child benefit, housing benefit and benefits for those who cannot work because of disability.

The term National Insurance Contribution is often shortened to NI or NIC. The type of National Insurance paid by employers and employees is referred to as being **Class 1** National Insurance.

To be eligible for a full state pension in the UK, individuals currently need to have 35 years of wages above the **lower earnings limit (LEL)** for NIC, which is currently £123 a week. Most employees will actually start having to make NI contributions when they earn over £242 a week (the primary threshold for 2023/24).

Employees pay Class 1 NIC which their employer is required to deduct from their pay. The amount deducted depends on how much of their earnings fall within certain bands.

Employers pay Class 1 NIC once the employee's pay exceeds £175 per week (£758 per month). For most employees this is paid at 13.8%.

Employers also pay Class 1A and Class 1B NIC on expenses and benefits that they give their employees. This is also paid at 13.8%.

All National Insurance calculations are made by the computerised payroll program, and the employee's NIC for the month, and the cumulative amount of NIC, will be shown on the employee's payslip.

It is very important that the information held on the payroll system about an employee is accurate and up-to-date to ensure these calculations are correct. We will look at the information on a payslip later in this chapter.

employment allowance

The **employment allowance** aims to encourage businesses to recruit staff by allowing eligible employers to reduce their NIC liability.

If a business or charity (including community amateur sports clubs) had employers' Class 1 National Insurance liabilities in the previous tax year of less than £100,000, it is eligible to claim **employment allowance**.

Employment allowance allows eligible employers to reduce their annual National Insurance liability by up to £5,000. The employer will pay less employers' Class 1 National Insurance each time it runs its payroll until the maximum of £5,000 has been used up, or the tax year ends (whichever is sooner).

The employer can only claim against its employers' Class 1 National Insurance liability up to a maximum of £5,000 each tax year but can still claim the allowance if its liability was less than £5,000 a year.

The claim for employment allowance is made on the Employer Payment Summary (EPS), which we will look at later in this chapter.

student loans

Students attending university or college can borrow amounts from the government to cover tuition fees and living expenses while they are studying. Once the student has finished their studying this loan amount is paid back through the payroll at 9% of pay above an annual earnings threshold set by the government. Employers are obliged to deduct this amount from the employee's pay and pay it to HMRC together with PAYE, NICs and other deductions.

pensions

Pensions are a way of saving for retirement. All employers must offer a workplace pension scheme, sometimes known as occupational, works, company, or work-based pensions. A percentage of the employee's pay is put into the pension scheme automatically every payday and in most cases, the employer must also contribute to the pension scheme. As we have seen earlier, the employee may get tax relief from the government on their pension contributions.

The workplace pension system is known as automatic enrolment. The employer must automatically enrol an employee into a pension scheme and make contributions to the pension if all of the following apply to the employee:

- they are classified as a worker
- they are aged between 22 and state pension age
- they earn at least £10,000 per year
- they usually work in the UK

There are also a number of other situations that mean an employer does not usually have to automatically enrol an employee in addition to them not meeting the above criteria. These can be found on the www.gov.uk website. It is worth noting that an employee can usually still join the pension scheme if they want to – the employer cannot refuse.

If an employee has been automatically enrolled the employer and employee must pay a percentage of the employee's earnings into the workplace pension scheme. The amount that is paid in depends on the pension scheme that the employer has chosen.

However, an employer has to pay a minimum of 3% of the employee's total earnings into the pension scheme and the employee must pay a minimum of 5%. This makes a total minimum contribution of 8%. Total earnings include:

- salary or wages

- bonuses and commission

- overtime

- statutory sick pay

- statutory maternity, paternity or adoption pay

In some schemes, the employer has the option to pay in more than the legal minimum. In these schemes, the employee can pay in less as long as the employer puts in enough to meet the total minimum contribution.

If an employee has **voluntarily** enrolled in a workplace pension, the employer must contribute the minimum amount if the employee earns more than:

- £520 a month

- £120 a week

- £480 over 4 weeks

But it does not have to contribute anything if the employee earns these amounts, or less.

non-statutory deductions

Employers may be required to make other deductions from gross pay for items such as:

- **charitable giving** – where an employee chooses to make a charitable donation through a charitable giving scheme. The donation will be deducted from the employee's gross pay before tax, but after NICs

- **union membership fees** – some trade union members pay their union subscriptions directly out of their pay and the employer then gives these payments to the union.

- **private medical insurance** – if an employee contributes to a private medical insurance scheme arranged through their employer, the employer must deduct this from the employee's pay, and pay it the insurance provider. The employer will often also contribute to the scheme. Employees do not get tax relief on these deductions

■ **savings schemes** – an employer may offer a saving scheme to its employees, where it deducts an amount from their pay and puts it into a savings scheme for them to access at a later date

The following example shows how much will be paid to each organisation when a monthly payroll is carried out.

Case Study

s i t u a t i o n

Viktor is responsible for the payroll at Feelux Ltd. He has prepared the wages report for September 2023, an extract from which is shown below.

	£
Gross pay	184,452.84
Income Tax	34,170.40
Employers' NIC	16,410.20
Employees' NIC	17,014.21
Employers' pension contributions	7,231.01
Employees' pension contributions	7,874.57
Employees' union fees	£820
Student loan repayments	£221.70

Calculate the total amounts due to employees, HMRC, pension provider and unions.

s o l u t i o n

	Amounts included	Calculation	Amount payable
Employees	Gross pay minus income tax, employees' NIC, employees' pension contributions, unions fees and student loan repayments	£184,452.84 – £34,170.40 – £17,014.21 – £7,874.57 – £820 – £221.70	£124,351.96
HMRC	Income Tax, employer's and employees' NIC, and student loan repayments	£34,170.40 + £16,410.20 + £17,014.21 + £221.70	£67,816.51
Pension provider	Employer's and employees' pension contributions	£7,231.01 + £7,874.57	£15,105.58
Unions	Employees' union fees	£820	£820

PAYROLL FORMS

As part of the payroll process employers are required to produce a variety of forms.

payslip

When an employer pays its employees, it must give each of them a payslip that shows details of how their net pay is calculated. The design of a payslip is not defined by law so there is a wide variety of payslips with different layouts and designs depending on the payroll software that a business uses. Examples of a monthly and a weekly payslip are shown below and on the next page.

example of a payslip – monthly paid

Employer details:	Plento Ltd, 4-7 Streetly Walk, Westly, ZX21 4SW				
Employee name:	Martina Farnago		Pay period:		Monthly
Employee number:	194753		Period number:		12
Payment method:	BACS Transfer		Pay date:		31 March 2023
NI number:	NH0123456F		Tax code:		1250L
		Deductions		Year-to-date balances	
Basic Pay:	2,000.00	PAYE Tax Paid:	176.72	PAYE Tax Paid:	2,120.64
Overtime:	0.00	Employee NIC:	114.30	Employee NIC:	1,740.00
		Pension – Employee:	100.00	Pension – Employee:	891.80
Total Pay:	**2,000.00**	Total deductions:	**391.02**	NET PAY	**1,603.88**

example of a payslip – weekly paid

Ref	Employee Name	Process Date	NI Number
1724	Mr Will Saunders	1/08/2023	PE347944C

Payments	Hours	Rate	Amount		Deductions	Amount
Basic	42.00	10.42	437.64		PAYE Tax	40.20
					National Insurance	23.48
					Pension	21.88
Holiday taken: 9.0		Remaining:	14.0			

Mr Will Saunders	This period		Year to date	
32 Brendan Street	Total Gross Pay	437.64	Total Gross Pay TD	7439.88
Wichworth	Gross for Tax	437.64	Gross for Tax TD	7439.88
WZ2 4QA			Tax Paid TD	682.40
	Earnings for NI	437.64	Earning for NI TD	7439.88
			National Insurance TD	399.16
	Payment Period	Weekly	Ee Pension TD	216.07
	Employer NI	0.00	Employer NI TD	0.00
	Er Pension TD	9.53	Er Pension TD	162.01

Regworth Ltd Tax code 1231L	Tax Period: 17	Payment method: BACS	Net Pay	352.08

The payslip must be provided to employees on, or before, their payday and can be a physical copy or sent electronically by email. Payslips must show:

- the gross amount of the wages or salary – before any deductions

- the amounts of any variable, and any fixed, deductions from that gross amount and the purposes for which they are made, for example PAYE, National Insurance, and pension contributions

- the net amount of wages or salary payable

- the number of hours

P45

When employees leave an employment, by law, the payroll department must issue them with a form called a **P45**. The P45 summarises information about the employee and their pay to date. As part of the leaving process, HMRC is informed online when the employer makes the final payment to an employee.

The employee must be given their copy of the P45 on the date their employment is terminated, or, with the employee's agreement, on the day their final wage payment is made.

A P45 has several parts:

Part 1A – the employee's copy

This is retained by the employee who is leaving.

Part 2 – copy for new employer

This contains some of the information included in the employee's copy and is given to the new employer together with Part 3.

Part 3 – completed by the new employer

Part 3 is a repeat of the information in Part 2 with space for the new employer to complete the bottom section, which gives details of the new employer's reference, name, and address along with the new employee's details for entry into the payroll records. This information is submitted online to HMRC when the new employee is paid for the first time by the new employer.

HMRC is advised that the employee is leaving as part of the final online submission of payroll information before the employee leaves.

It is worth noting that the P45 **does not** include any details of NICs.

The new employer will use the information in parts 2 and 3 to set up a new employee record for the new starter on the computerised payroll system.

On the next page is a blank Part 1A of a P45 form.

HM Revenue & Customs

P45 Part 1A
Details of employee leaving work
Copy for employee

1 Employer PAYE reference

Office number *Reference number*

[   ] / [   ]

2 Employee's National Insurance number

[   ]

3 Title - enter MR, MRS, MISS, MS or other title

[   ]

Surname or family name

[   ]

First or given name(s)

[   ]

4 Leaving date *DD MM YYYY*

[   ] [   ] [   ]

5 Student Loan deductions

[   ] Student Loan deductions to continue

6 Tax Code at leaving date

[   ]

If week 1 or month 1 applies, enter 'X' in the box below.

Week 1/Month 1 [   ]

7 Last entries on P11 *Deductions Working Sheet.*
Complete only if Tax Code is cumulative. If there is an 'X' at box 6 there will be no entries here.

Week number [   ]   Month number [   ]

Total pay to date

£ [   ] p

Total tax to date

£ [   ] p

8 This employment pay and tax. If no entry here, the amounts are those shown at box 7.

Total pay in this employment

£ [   ] p

Total tax in this employment

£ [   ] p

9 Works number/Payroll number and Department or branch (if any)

[   ]

10 Gender. Enter 'X' in the appropriate box

Male [   ]   Female [   ]

11 Date of birth *DD MM YYYY*

[   ] [   ] [   ]

12 Employee's private address

[   ]

Postcode

[   ]

13 I certify that the details entered in items 1 to 11 on this form are correct.

Employer name and address

[   ]

Postcode

[   ]

Date *DD MM YYYY*

[   ] [   ] [   ]

To the employee
The P45 is in three parts. Please keep this part (Part1A) safe. Copies are not available. You might need the information in Part 1A to fill in a Tax Return if you are sent one.

Please read the notes in Part 2 that accompany Part 1A. The notes give some important information about what you should do next and what you should do with Parts 2 and 3 of this form.

Tax Credits
Tax credits are flexible. They adapt to changes in your life, such as leaving a job. If you need to let us know about a change in your income, phone **0845 300 3900**.

To the new employer
If your new employee gives you this Part 1A, please return it to them. Deal with Parts 2 and 3 as normal.

P45(Online) Part 1 A

HMRC 10/08

P60

A form **P60** shows the tax an employee has paid in the tax year (6 April to 5 April). Any employee who works more than one job will get a separate P60 for each job.

If the employee is working for an employer on 5 April the employer must give them a P60 by 31st May, on paper, or electronically.

An employee needs their P60 to prove how much tax they've paid on their salary. This will be necessary for the following:

■ to claim back overpaid tax

■ to apply for tax credits

■ as proof of income if the employee applies for a loan or a mortgage

Below is an example of a P60.

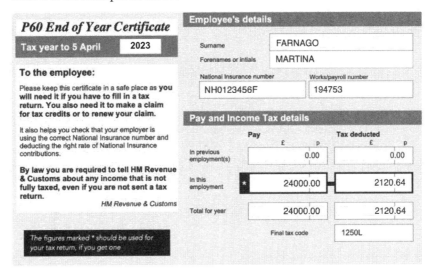

P11D

A form P11D is used to tell HMRC about any benefits in kind that the employee has received, for example a company car, health insurance or gym membership. These 'benefits in kind' effectively increase the employee's taxable pay, so a P11D must be submitted to HMRC for each employee who has been provided with expenses or benefits in the tax year.

An employer must submit P11D forms online to HMRC by 6th July after the end of the tax year to which they relate, and because these benefits form part of the employee's pay, the employer must pay NIC on them – referred to as **Class 1A NIC**. They must also provide a copy of the P11D to each employee by the same date. The employer must then pay any Class 1A National Insurance it owes by 22nd July.

Below is an example of a P11D.

G Vans and van fuel

Total cash equivalent or amount foregone for all vans made available in 2020 to 2021 — **9** £ `1A`

Total cash equivalent or amount foregone on fuel for all vans made available in 2020 to 2021 — **10** £ `1A`

H Interest-free and low interest loans

If the total amount outstanding on all loans does not exceed £10,000 at any time in the year, there's no need to complete this section unless the loan is provided under an optional remuneration arrangement when the threshold does not apply

	Loan 1	Loan 2
Number of joint borrowers if applicable		
Amount outstanding at 5 April 2020 or at date loan was made if later	£	£
Amount outstanding at 5 April 2021 or at date loan was discharged if earlier	£	£
Maximum amount outstanding at any time in the year	£	£
Total amount of interest paid by the borrower in 2020 to 2021 enter 'NIL' if none was paid	£	£
Date loan was made in 2020 to 2021 if applicable	/ /	/ /
Date loan was discharged in 2020 to 2021 if applicable	/ /	/ /
Cash equivalent or relevant amount of loans after deducting any interest paid by the borrower	**15** £ `1A`	**15** £ `1A`

I Private medical treatment or insurance

	Cost to you or amount foregone	Amount made good or from which tax deducted	Cash equivalent or relevant amount
Private medical treatment or insurance	£	– £	= **11** £ `1A`

J Qualifying relocation expenses payments and benefits

Non-qualifying benefits and expenses go in sections M and N below

Excess over £8,000 of all qualifying relocation expenses payments and benefits for each move — **15** £ `1A`

K Services supplied

	Cost to you or amount foregone	Amount made good or from which tax deducted	Cash equivalent or relevant amount
Services supplied to the employee	£	– £	= **15** £ `1A`

L Assets placed at the employee's disposal

	Cost of the benefit or amount foregone	Amount made good or from which tax deducted	Cash equivalent or relevant amount
Description of asset	£	– £	= **13** £ `1A`

M Other items (including subscriptions and professional fees)

	Cost to you or amount foregone	Amount made good or from which tax deducted	Cash equivalent or relevant amount
Description of other items	£	– £	= **15** £ `1A`
Description of other items	£	– £	= **15** £

Income Tax paid but not deducted from director's remuneration — Tax paid **15** £

N Expenses payments made on behalf of the employee

	Cost to you or amount foregone	Amount made good or from which tax deducted	Taxable payment or relevant amount
Travelling and subsistence payments - Cost to you or amount foregone except mileage allowance payments for employee's own car, read section E	£	– £	= **16** £
Entertainment - Cost to you or amount foregone trading organisations read P11D Guide and then enter a tick or a cross as appropriate here	£	– £	= **16** £
Payments for use of home telephone	£	– £	= **16** £
Non-qualifying relocation expenses those not shown in sections J or M	£	– £	= **16** £
Description of other expenses	£	– £	= **16** £

Return all your form P11Ds and one P11D(b) by 6 July 2021 to:
P11D Support Team, BP2302, HM Revenue and Customs, Department 1250, Newcastle upon Tyne, NE98 1ZZ

REPORTING TO HMRC

As we have seen earlier in this chapter, employers are required to submit payroll details to HMRC online in real time (RTI) via approved computerised payroll software on, or before, each payday.

full payment submission (FPS)

Payroll software is used to submit a **Full Payment Submission (FPS).** This tells HMRC about payments employers have made to employees and deductions that have been made. The FPS should include everyone who is paid, and **must be submitted on, or before, payday**.

The FPS must be sent to HMRC before the employees' payday, even if the business is permitted to actually pay HMRC quarterly instead of monthly (see page 131 for more details).

The FPS should include the usual date that employees are paid, even if they are paid earlier or later, for example, due to a bank holiday. The FPS can be sent before the regular payday, for example if payroll staff are going on leave, but should not be reported too early as a corrected FPS would need to be sent to advise HMRC if any information changes – for example if an employee leaves or there is a change to an employee's tax code. Reports for a new tax year cannot be sent before March.

completing and sending an FPS

The employer's PAYE reference and accounts office reference will need to be entered into the payroll software which will then provide instructions that guide the employer (or payroll bureau) on how to complete the FPS.

HMRC has guidance on what to put in each field on an FPS, including:

■ **employer information**: HMRC office number, employer PAYE number, accounts office reference, tax year

■ **employee information**: (for every employee paid in the period only) National Insurance number, full name and title, date of birth, gender, address with postcode, country of residence – if they live outside the UK, payroll ID – if the employer has assigned one, irregular payroll pattern – if the employee is not being paid regularly (eg if they do casual work)

■ **pay and deductions**: (for every employee paid in the period only) for the period and for the tax year to date taxable pay, tax deducted or refunded, student loan repayment recovered, pay after statutory deductions (tax, NICs and student loans), other deductions from net pay, pension deductions, statutory maternity, paternity, adoption, and shared parental pay

- **employee pay information**: (for each payment made to an employee) employee tax code, employee hours normally worked, pay frequency, payment date, tax week number, tax month number
- **National Insurance**: (for employees who earn more than £120 per week) National Insurance letter, gross earnings for National Insurance Contributions in this period and year to date, earnings at the lower earnings limit, primary threshold, and upper earnings limit for the year to date, employee NI Contributions payable this period and year to date, total of employer's contributions payable in this pay period and year to date

Additional information will need to be included on an FPS in the following circumstances:

- a **new employee** – when a new employee joins a business, their details must be included on **the next FPS**. This will include personal information collected from them and from their P45 if they were previously employed, the tax code that the new employer has worked out for them, their starter declaration, and pay and deductions (for example tax, National Insurance and student loan deductions) since they started working for the new employer – do not include figures from their previous job
- an **employee leaves**: the employee's leaving date should be included on their payroll record and deductions should be made as normal when the next FPS is submitted. The employer must also issue them with a P45

employer payment summary (EPS)

In the following tax month (starting on the 6th) after an employer has submitted its FPS, the employer can log into its HMRC online account and view its FPS. From the 12th of the tax month it will be able to see how much tax and National Insurance it owes in its HMRC online account.

An **Employer Payment Summary (EPS)** needs to be sent by the 19th of the following tax month, to apply for any reduction on what the employer owes on its FPS. An example might be statutory sick pay, which is a basic amount of sick pay paid to employees that the employer can claim back from HMRC. The employer will also claim for the **Employment Allowance** of up to £5,000 on the EPS (employment status was covered in detail on page 117).

If an employer has not actually paid any employees in the tax month, then it should send an EPS instead of an FPS.

penalties for late submission of payroll filings

An employer who fails to make an FPS on time, or does not file an EPS, may be liable to pay the following:

1 **A monthly penalty** as shown in the table below, based on the number of employees. No penalty will arise for the first month in each tax year where there is a filing default. This means there is a maximum of 11 penalties per tax year that can be charged for filing failures.

Number of employees	Monthly penalty
1 to 9	£100
10 to 49	£200
50 to 249	£300
250 or more	£400

2 **An estimate of any amount due to HMRC** (where applicable), based on previous submissions, plus interest.

Normally, HMRC will send employers a filing penalty notice quarterly in July, October, January, and April. These penalty notices show the amount of the filing penalty for each tax month identified in that quarter. For example, a penalty notice in July will show any filing penalties arising in the first quarter of the tax year – that is, month 1 (6 Apr to 5 May), month 2 (6 May to 5 June) and month 3 (6 June to 5 July). There are additional penalties for returns over three months late.

All penalties are due for payment within 30 days of the date of the penalty notice. Penalties that are not paid on time will attract interest.

Penalties may not apply:

- if the FPS is late but all reported payments on the late FPS are made within three days of the employees' payday. However, if the business is regularly late submitting, the penalty may still be charged

- where a new employer sends their first FPS late, but it is still within 30 days of paying an employee

- if it is an employer's first failure in the tax year to send a report on time

penalties for inaccuracies in payroll filings

If there are inaccuracies in the payroll submissions that a business makes, it may be subject to penalties. The amount of these penalties will depend on whether the inaccuracy was careless (simply a mistake), deliberate (the employee knew there was a mistake such as paying wages without accounting for PAYE and NIC), or deliberate and concealed (the employer not only know the return was inaccurate, but also took steps to hide this, for example recording lower numbers of hours worked than was actually paid).

The level of the penalty will also be affected by whether the disclosure of the error was unprompted (the employer tells HMRC about the error before it has any reason to believe HMRC is going to find it) or prompted (any other time).

An employer can be charged a penalty which is a percentage of the potential lost revenue (PLR) for HMRC. The percentage penalties are shown in the table below:

Type of behaviour	Unprompted disclosure	Prompted disclosure
	%	%
Careless	0-30	15-30
Deliberate	20-70	35-70
Deliberate and concealed	30-100	50-100

PAYING HMRC

monthly payroll payments

Tax and NICs deducted from employees' pay plus employers' NICs due, and any student loan deductions, are payable to HMRC on a monthly basis regardless of the frequency of the payroll. Employers have to pay the tax and National Insurance reported on their Full Payment Submission (FPS) that was submitted in the previous tax month, minus any reductions detailed on an EPS (if they sent one before the 19th in the current tax month). The employer must then pay what it owes by the 22nd of each month, if paid electronically, or the 19th if paying by post.

For example, if a business has a payday of 25th September, this falls in the tax month 6th September to 5th October.

- The FPS for this payroll must be submitted on or before 25th September
- The EPS must be submitted by 19th October

- Payment must be received by HMRC by 22nd October if it is paid electronically, or 19th October if it is paid by post

A small employer that usually pays less than £1,500 per month may be able to pay quarterly instead of monthly, but it will need to contact HMRC to see if it is eligible.

penalties for late monthly/quarterly payroll payments

If payments are missed or received late, HMRC applies a range of penalties, with the amount depending on how many there are.

The first failure to pay on time is not treated as a default and so does not attract a penalty, but subsequent late or non-payments do, as shown in the table below.

Number of defaults in a tax year	Penalty percentage applied to the amount that is late in the relevant tax month
1 to 3	1%
4 to 6	2%
7 to 9	3%
10 or more	4%

The penalty percentage is applied to the total amount that is late in the relevant tax month.

HMRC will send filing penalty notices quarterly in July, October, January, and April. These penalty notices show the amount of the filing penalty for each tax month identified in that quarter. For example, a penalty notice in July will show any filing penalties arising in the first quarter of the tax year – that is, month 1 (6 Apr to 5 May), month 2 (6 May to 5 June) and month 3 (6 June to 5 July).

Additional penalties will apply as follows:

- A monthly or quarterly amount remains outstanding after six months: the penalty will be 5% of the unpaid tax

- A monthly or quarterly amount remains outstanding after 12 months: the penalty will be a further 5% of the unpaid tax ie a total of 10%

These additional penalties apply even when only one payment in the tax year is late.

PAYE settlement agreements

A **PAYE Settlement Agreement (PSA)** allows an employer to make one annual payment to cover all the tax and National Insurance due on 'minor or irregular' benefits that they give to their employees.

Minor benefits and expense payments include: incentive awards (for example for long-service), telephone bills, small gifts and vouchers, staff entertainment (for example a ticket to an event), and non-business expenses while travelling overnight on business that are over the daily limit of £5 per night in the UK and £10 per night outside the UK.

Irregular benefits and expenses are things that are not paid at regular intervals over the course of a tax year, ie not weekly or monthly, and are not included in an employee's contract.

An example of irregular benefits might be the costs of paying for a staff outing to celebrate a successful product launch.

If an employer gets a PSA for these items, it will **not** need to:

- put them through its payroll to work out tax and NICs

- include them in its year-end P11D forms

- pay Class 1A NICs on them at the end of the tax year as it will pay Class 1B National Insurance as part of the PSA instead

The deadline for applying for a PSA is the 5th July following the first tax year to which it applies.

So, for the tax year 2023 to 2024 an employer will have until 5 July 2024 to apply for a PSA. This gives the employer time to identify whether it has expenses and benefits that fall into any of the categories that qualify.

Any tax and National Insurance owed under a PSA must be paid by 22nd October following the tax year to which the PSA applies (payment must be by 19th October if it is made by post).

late payment of amounts due annually or occasionally

An employer may have to pay a penalty if it has not paid the full amount by the date known as the 'penalty date'. In most cases the penalty date is the day after the due date for payment. However, for payments of NICs on benefits, the 'penalty date' is 30 days after the due date. Employers may have to pay:

- 5% penalty if the full amount is not paid within 30 days of the due date

- an additional 5% penalty if the full amount is not paid within 6 months

- a further 5% penalty if the full amount is not paid within 12 months

Chapter Summary

- Any business or individual that employs people must register with HMRC as an employer before the first payday.

- employers are required to run their payrolls using computerised payroll software which transmits up-to-date payroll information electronically to HMRC in a process called Real Time Information (RTI).

- A business should ensure that it updates its payroll software from 6 April, or earlier if the software provider asks it to.

- Employers must keep payroll records for three years after the end of the tax year to which they relate.

- Employers must comply with data protection principles when dealing with personal information about their employees.

- HMRC is entitled to check the PAYE records of all employees.

- The PAYE system calculates and applies deductions for Income Tax in the UK. Income Tax is a direct tax that is paid on taxable income over a certain threshold. The amount of tax that an employee pays on their earnings is determined by their tax code.

- Employers are required by law to make statutory deductions, such as tax, National Insurance and student loan repayments, from their employees' pay.

- National Insurance Contributions are due from employees and employers on the employee's pay over a threshold.

- Employees must authorise any non-statutory (voluntary) deductions from their pay, eg charity donations, pension contributions and subscriptions. Some voluntary deductions attract tax relief.

- An employer that had class 1 National Insurance liabilities in the previous tax year of less than £100,000 is eligible to claim Employment Allowance which will cover up to £5,000 of its current year's employer's NIC liability.

- Employers must provide their employees with a payslip each time they pay them, showing the gross amount, all deductions, and the net pay.

- When employees leave an employment, the payroll department must, by law, issue them with a P45 on the day their employment is terminated. A copy of the P45 must be given to the person's new employer.

- A P60 shows the tax an employee has paid in the tax year (6 April to 5 April). Employees need their P60 to prove how much tax they've paid on their salary.

■ An employer must submit P11D forms about any expenses or benefits that the employee has received and the total Class 1A National Insurance it owes on this, which must be paid by 22nd July. It must also provide a copy of the P11D to each employee by 6th July.

■ Employers must make a Full Payment Submission (FPS) which tells HMRC about payments to employees and deductions that have been made. The FPS should include everyone who is paid, and must be submitted on, or before, payday.

■ If an employer has not actually paid any employees in the tax month, then it should submit an Employer Payment Summary (EPS) by the 19th of the following tax month. The employer will also claim for the Employment Allowance on its EPS.

■ Employers that fail to submit an FPS or an EPS may be liable for a penalty which is based on the number of employees and the amount due to HMRC.

■ Employers may be subject to penalties if the payroll submissions they make are inaccurate, depending on whether they were careless, deliberate, or deliberate and concealed.

■ Employers should pay what they owe to HMRC electronically by 22nd of each month (19th if payment is made by post). HMRC may charge the employer penalties if payment is late.

■ A PAYE Settlement Agreement (PSA) allows an employer to make one annual payment to cover all the tax and National Insurance due on 'minor, irregular or impracticable' expenses or benefits that it gives to its employees.

RTI	Real Time Information – the process of updating HMRC online using computerised payroll software
gross pay	total pay before any statutory or voluntary deductions
free pay	pay that is not subject to Income Tax
tax code	a combination of a number and a letter representing how much free pay an employee is entitled to. Each employee has a tax code
taxable pay	the amount on which Income Tax is payable by an employee
tax relief	relief given on some deductions from payroll such as pension contributions or charitable donations. Tax is not charged on the pay used to make these payments
net pay	the amount an employee receives after all deductions
PAYE	Pay As You Earn – HMRC's system for collecting Income Tax and National Insurance from employees
NIC	National Insurance Contributions – paid to government by employees and employers to fund state benefits
National Insurance number	a combination of letters and numbers in a given number format, unique to each worker in the UK. A person is identified by the same NI number throughout their life
Class 1 NIC	National Insurance Contributions made by employees and employers once the employee's pay exceeds a threshold
Class 1A & Class 1B NIC	National Insurance Contributions paid by employers on expenses and benefits that they give their employees
LEL	lower earnings limit – the level below which no NIC is due, and no benefit accrued
student loans	a government loan to individuals to cover college or university costs, repayable through the payroll

employment allowance	an allowance for smaller employers to reduce their annual National Insurance Contributions by up to £5,000
P45	an official form containing personal and employment data which must be completed by an employer and handed to an employee when they leave that employment
P60	an official form that shows the tax an employee has paid on their earnings in the tax year
P11D	an official form that tells HMRC about expenses and benefits an employee has received in the year
FPS	Full Payment Submission - online submission of pay information to HMRC on, or before, a pay day
EPS	Employer Payment Summary – online submission to apply to reduce what the employer owes on its FPS and to claim employment allowance. An EPS should still be submitted if the employer has not actually paid anyone in the tax month
PAYE settlement agreement	an agreement with HMRC that allows an employer to make one annual payment to cover all the tax and National Insurance due on 'minor, irregular or impracticable' expenses or benefits that they give to their employees

Activities

5.1 Decide which of the following are correct in relation to registering as an employer.

(a)	They must register if they employ more than three people	
(b)	They must register before the first pay day	
(c)	They can register up to six months before they start paying employees	
(d)	They must run their payroll using computerised payroll software	
(e)	Individuals who employ staff are required to register as an employer	

Select **all** options that are correct.

5.2 The abbreviation RTI stands for which of the following?

(a)	Regular Time Integration	
(b)	Real Time Information	
(c)	Real Transfer Information	
(d)	Required Transfer Information	

Select **one** option that is correct.

5.3 Complete the following statement by selecting the correct words from the options available.

'HMRC [**is / is not**] entitled to visit an employer's premises to check its payroll records. If the employer has paid too much it will receive a refund and will [**always / sometimes / never**] be paid interest on this refund. If the business has not paid enough, it will be asked to pay the additional amount within [**seven / 30 / 60**] days. HMRC will [**sometimes / always**] charge the employer a penalty if it has underpaid.'

5.4   Match each of the definitions below to the payroll term to which they relate.

Definition	Payroll term
Tax on deductions from an employee's gross pay on which tax is not due.	
The amount an employee receives after all deductions.	
An employee's total earnings after any tax-free deductions.	
An employee's total earnings before any deductions.	
A combination of a number and a letter representing how much free pay an employee is entitled to.	

Payroll terms: Taxable pay; Tax code; Tax relief: Gross pay: Net pay

5.5   Identify whether each of the following deductions from an employee's pay is statutory or non-statutory.

Deduction	Statutory deduction	Non-statutory deduction
Student loan		
PAYE		
Union subscriptions		
Employee's National Insurance Contribution		
Pension		
Donation to charity		
Private medical insurance		

5.6 Ludo has received his payslip which shows his net pay for the month as £1,760. He knows that he worked 164 hours in the month and his pay rate is £13.22 per hour. He has asked you to explain why he has not received the full amount that he's earned.

Identify which of the following may have caused the difference between what Ludo earned and what he received. Tick **all** the correct options.

Option	May have caused the difference
PAYE	
Union subscription	
Employee's National Insurance Contribution	
Employer's National Insurance Contribution	
Employer's pension contribution	
Employee's pension contribution	
Charitable donation	
Private medical insurance	

5.7 **(a)** What is the maximum amount an employer's Class 1 National Insurance Contributions for the previous year can be for them to be eligible for employment allowance for the current year?

£ [   ]

(b) What is the maximum reduction in Class 1 NIC an employer can get if it is eligible for Employment Allowance?

£ [   ]

(c) On which form should an employer claim employment allowance?

[   ]

5.8 Match each of the definitions below to the payroll document to which they relate.

Definition	Payroll term
The form that tells HMRC about expenses and benefits an employee has received in the year.	
The form that shows the tax an employee has paid on their earnings in the tax year.	
The online submission that should be made if the employer has not actually paid anyone in the tax month.	
The online submission of pay information to HMRC on, or before, a pay day.	
The form that the employer gives to an employee who leaves employment with them. It contains personal and employment data and has a part that needs to be given to the individual's new employer.	

Payroll documents: P45; P60; P11D; Full Payment Submission (FPS); Employer Payment Summary (EPS)

5.9 A PAYE settlement agreement allows an employer to make one annual payment for which of the following?

(a)	PAYE on the wages of employees paid monthly	
(b)	NIC on benefits in kind	
(c)	Tax and NIC on 'minor, irregular or impracticable' expenses or benefits given to employees	
(d)	PAYE on the wages of employees paid weekly	

5.10 Josh has already made four late payroll payments to HMRC in the tax year. What percentage will be applied to the amount of the 5th late payment?

(a)	1%	
(b)	2%	
(c)	3%	
(d)	4%	

Which **one** of these options is correct?

5.11 Georgeard Ltd, a manufacturing business in the UK that employs 237 members of staff, has failed to file its Full Payment Submission (FPS) on time for the second time this tax year. What will be the penalty for this?

(a)	£200	
(b)	£300	
(c)	£2,000	
(d)	£3,000	

Which **one** of these options is correct?

5.12 Nikita works as an assistant accountant at Resolvase Ltd. He has prepared the wages report for the quarter ended December 2023, an extract from which is shown below.

	£
Gross wages	21,234.10
Income Tax	1,078.22
Employer's NIC	1,014.21
Employees' NIC	733.01
Employment allowance	322.14

Complete the following information about the payroll information.

The amount due to HMRC is	£
The date the amount must be paid by is	
The business can pay quarterly as its average monthly PAYE payment is less than	£

6 Communicating VAT and payroll information

this chapter covers...

This chapter describes the way in which information about VAT and payroll should be communicated to:

- *managers and staff of a business*

- *clients of an accounting practice*

The areas in which VAT and payroll information must be communicated internally within the business include:

- *providing relevant information to the appropriate person, including details of amounts due, time limits for submission of returns, and making payment and requesting authorisation*

- *informing managers about the way in which payment of VAT to HMRC by the business will affect the cash flow and financial forecasts of the business*

- *informing managers and staff about other changes in VAT and payroll legislation*

- *informing managers and staff about what happens when the rate of VAT changes on a certain date and how this affects operations such as invoicing*

The chapter also looks at the need for accountants to behave ethically when dealing with VAT and payroll.

Lastly, the chapter describes the way in which a business communicates with HMRC.

REPORTING INFORMATION

reporting to the relevant person

The previous chapters of this book have focussed on the processes that an accountant in practice or in business goes through to prepare accurate and timely submissions for VAT and payroll. However, it is important that any information that is prepared is reported to the appropriate person within the organisation.

The work of a junior member of staff who prepares VAT Returns for clients of an accountancy practice, or for the business they work for, will normally be checked by a more senior member of staff to ensure that it is accurate. If the VAT Return is for a client, the accountant will normally advise the client of the amount of VAT that is due to HMRC, ie the Box 5 figure on the draft VAT Return, and the date by which this amount needs to be paid.

If the accountant works in business and has prepared the VAT Return for the business they work for, the same information must be communicated to the owner or appropriate manager of the business before the VAT Return can be submitted.

Where an accountant is responsible for running the payroll for the business they work for, they must ensure that the wages reports are provided to the appropriate person(s). For example, the accountant will need to be provided with the wages report in order to prepare the year-end accounts.

The wages report and the payroll will need to be approved before payroll submissions are made to HMRC and payment is made to employees, HMRC and other organisations such as pension providers or trade unions.

communicating time limits

We have already seen that there are strict deadlines for submission of VAT and payroll information to HMRC and for making payments. Failure to comply with these time limits may result in a business, or a client of an accounting practice, being faced with significant penalties and/or fines. This means that communication with management or clients must clearly state the latest date by which submissions must be made to avoid incurring any penalties.

gaining authorisation

If an accountancy practice prepares VAT Returns for its clients, it would be easy to think the practice could simply submit the returns, inform the client of the amount it needs to pay HMRC (or in some cases the amount it can reclaim from HMRC), and tell the client the date the payment needs to be made. However, in addition to providing this information to the client, it is important that the VAT Return is not submitted until authorisation has been received from the client. Businesses that prepare their own VAT Returns must also ensure that they are reviewed and approved before they are submitted to HMRC.

As we saw in Chapter 5, payroll submissions are made in RTI, but before they are submitted, they must be reviewed and approved by a more senior line manager or by the client if they have been prepared by an accountancy practice or payroll bureau.

Case Study

Ramzi works as an assistant accountant at Somersby and Doyle, a medium sized accountancy practice. He has prepared the draft VAT Return for a client, The Roundhouse Restaurant, for the quarter ended August 2023, and a summary of the figures is shown here:

	£
Box 1	7,949.00
Box 4	2,912.45
Box 6	39,745
Box 7	18,245

Ramzi's manager has asked him to prepare an email to the owner of The Roundhouse containing the necessary information and asking for authorisation to submit the VAT Return to HMRC.

solution

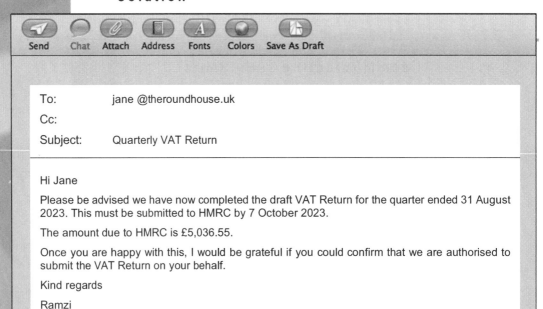

Send	Chat	Attach	Address	Fonts	Colors	Save As Draft

To: jane @theroundhouse.uk

Cc:

Subject: Quarterly VAT Return

Hi Jane

Please be advised we have now completed the draft VAT Return for the quarter ended 31 August 2023. This must be submitted to HMRC by 7 October 2023.

The amount due to HMRC is £5,036.55.

Once you are happy with this, I would be grateful if you could confirm that we are authorised to submit the VAT Return on your behalf.

Kind regards

Ramzi

VAT AND THE CASH FLOW OF A BUSINESS

the timing of VAT payments

The timing of VAT payments can have a significant effect on the cash flow of a business.

Normally a VAT-registered business will complete its VAT Return quarterly online. The VAT Return will have to be submitted online within one month and seven days of the end of the VAT period, and payment will be collected three working days later. If the customers of the business pay their invoices promptly the business will be able to bank these receipts – which include output VAT charged – and use this money as 'working capital' until it has to be paid to HMRC when the VAT Return is due.

Suppose, for example:

■ a consignment of goods is invoiced in mid-January

■ the invoice is paid in mid-February and the money is banked

■ the VAT quarter runs from 1 January to 31 March

■ the VAT Return and payment are due by 7 May

The business will then have the use of the VAT money due for at least two and a half months until the VAT payment is made in the first week of May. The timeline looks like this:

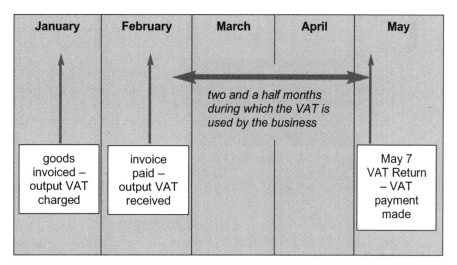

If this happened every VAT quarter, the business would receive a regular and useful boost to its working capital.

the effect on the cash budget

The situation described on the previous page would also be reflected in the company's cash budget, which would show:

- the output VAT charged to credit customers as part of the regular **monthly** cash inflow

- the **quarterly** payments to HMRC as cash outflows in May, August, November, and February

- the increased bank balance which results from the lag in making the quarterly payments to HMRC

further improvements to cash flow – some emails

In the email shown below, Tariq, an Accounts Supervisor, suggests to John Turner, his manager, that even tighter credit control would further improve the company's cash flow.

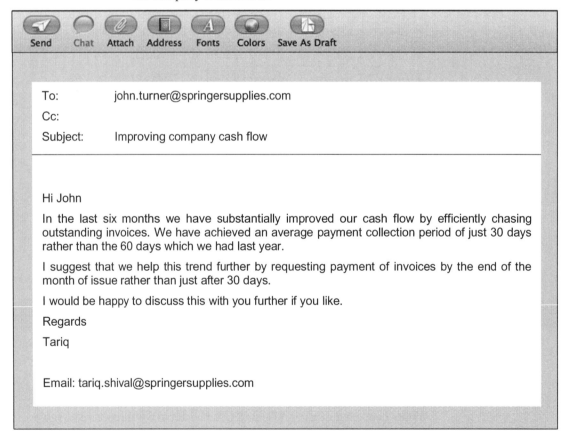

Send   Chat   Attach   Address   Fonts   Colors   Save As Draft

To: john.turner@springersupplies.com

Cc:

Subject: Improving company cash flow

Hi John

In the last six months we have substantially improved our cash flow by efficiently chasing outstanding invoices. We have achieved an average payment collection period of just 30 days rather than the 60 days which we had last year.

I suggest that we help this trend further by requesting payment of invoices by the end of the month of issue rather than just after 30 days.

I would be happy to discuss this with you further if you like.

Regards

Tariq

Email: tariq.shival@springersupplies.com

John Turner then replies as follows:

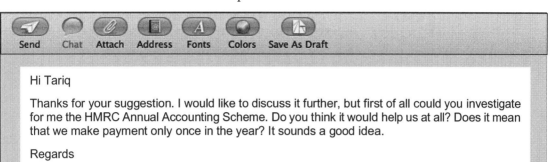

Hi Tariq

Thanks for your suggestion. I would like to discuss it further, but first of all could you investigate for me the HMRC Annual Accounting Scheme. Do you think it would help us at all? Does it mean that we make payment only once in the year? It sounds a good idea.

Regards

John

Tariq then looks into this and finds that the idea is not such a good one because payments have to be made more than once a year. He replies as follows:

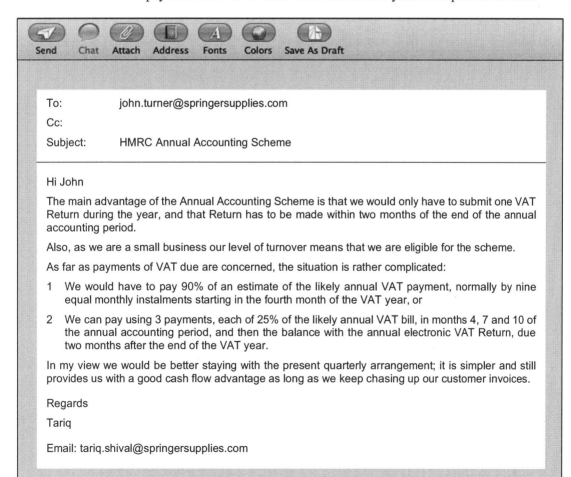

To: john.turner@springersupplies.com

Cc:

Subject: HMRC Annual Accounting Scheme

Hi John

The main advantage of the Annual Accounting Scheme is that we would only have to submit one VAT Return during the year, and that Return has to be made within two months of the end of the annual accounting period.

Also, as we are a small business our level of turnover means that we are eligible for the scheme.

As far as payments of VAT due are concerned, the situation is rather complicated:

1   We would have to pay 90% of an estimate of the likely annual VAT payment, normally by nine equal monthly instalments starting in the fourth month of the VAT year, or

2   We can pay using 3 payments, each of 25% of the likely annual VAT bill, in months 4, 7 and 10 of the annual accounting period, and then the balance with the annual electronic VAT Return, due two months after the end of the VAT year.

In my view we would be better staying with the present quarterly arrangement; it is simpler and still provides us with a good cash flow advantage as long as we keep chasing up our customer invoices.

Regards

Tariq

Email: tariq.shival@springersupplies.com

VAT and cash flow – conclusion

The exchange of emails on the last two pages shows how VAT information can be effectively communicated between members of a business team. In this case the points covered include:

- the cash flow advantage of having money in the bank because payment to HMRC is made over a month after the end of the VAT period – and sales invoices are settled promptly some months before

- the features of the annual accounting scheme for VAT which involves the annual submission of the VAT Return, but complex arrangements for payment of the VAT due to HMRC during the year

LEGISLATION

what is VAT law?

The law affects businesses by setting out principles which dictate what the businesses should, or should not, do when carrying out their everyday business.

The principles of VAT law originate from a number of different sources:

- the **Value Added Tax Act 1994** passed by the UK Parliament and amended from time to time in the various **Finance Acts** which turn Budget measures into legal requirements

- UK **statutory instruments** – these are detailed rules and regulations which have the authority of Acts of Parliament, but do not have to go through the lengthy processes required for passing an Act of Parliament

- certain **VAT Notices** published by HMRC and available on www.gov.uk

Navigating VAT law can be complicated; however, HMRC can normally provide the answer to most legal queries relating to VAT.

changes in VAT regulations

VAT regulations change frequently, most importantly in the period following the **Budget**. VAT rates are also subject to variation from time to time.

All these changes have significant effects on the running of businesses, for example:

- **VAT rate changes** affect the calculation of output VAT and the total prices on invoices, credit notes, price lists and price labels on goods; a rate change and its timing will also affect claims for input tax

- changes in the **types of goods and services that are chargeable to VAT** and the rates charged, for example the extension of reduced rate VAT to child car seats and domestic fuel

■ the introduction of new **VAT special schemes** and the modification of the upper turnover limit on existing schemes may affect how a business accounts for VAT

When there are changes to VAT legislation or regulation, specific timescales for the changes to be applied must be adhered to.

In this chapter we describe how a business deals with these changes and communicates the necessary information to the right people.

payroll legislation

Much of the detail on payroll legislation has already been covered in Chapter 5. However, it is important to reiterate the need to keep up-to-date with the latest payroll legislation. As we have seen, businesses are required to submit their payroll to HMRC in real time (RTI) using recognised accounting software, or using a payroll bureau to provide their payroll function. Payroll bureaus will ensure that they, and their clients, are complying with current payroll legislation.

However, if a business runs its own payroll, it is the responsibility of the business owners or managers to make sure they keep up-to-date with the most current legislation, and that the payroll software is updated regularly. An example of payroll legislation that changes each year is the national minimum wage rate and the national living wage. Employers must ensure that they are paying their staff above the appropriate minimum amounts which increase on an annual basis. Details of this will be available from the HMRC website and from the payroll software provider.

CHANGING THE VAT RATE

The most common and far-reaching change to the VAT system is a change in VAT rate. Zero rate, by definition, will not vary and the reduced rate VAT has been 5% for a number of years. Standard rate VAT, however, is subject to change, and when it does change it affects the great majority of businesses.

The normal reason for a change is government policy which may need to:

■ increase or decrease consumer spending in the economy – an increase, for example, will discourage spending

■ increase tax revenue for the government – an increase in VAT rate will help to fund government spending

For businesses, however, the changes brought about by a change in VAT rate will be more immediate.

DEALING WITH AN INCREASE IN THE STANDARD VAT RATE

Let's use an example: suppose the UK government announced an increase in standard rate VAT by 2% to take effect on 1 April.

This means that for any sales of standard-rated goods or services made on, or after, 1 April, a business must charge VAT at the new, increased rate. This change only applies to the standard VAT rate. There are no changes to sales that are zero-rated or reduced-rated for VAT. There are also no changes to VAT-exempt supplies.

So, how does this affect businesses?

retailers

If the business is a **retailer,** it must use the increased rate for all takings received on, or after, 1 April. If the customer paid after 1 April for something it received before 1 April, this means that the sale took place before 1 April and the earlier, lower rate should be used.

businesses that sell on credit

If the business issues **VAT invoices**, it must use the increased rate for all VAT invoices issued on, or after, 1 April. If a business provided goods or services before 1 April and issued a VAT invoice after that date, a business can choose to account for VAT at the earlier, lower rate.

special rules for services

If a business provides **services** that started **before** 1 April but finished **after** that date, it may invoice for the work done up to 31 March at the lower rate and the remainder at the higher rate.

continuous supplies of services

If a business provides **continuous services** such as the leasing of office equipment, it should account for the VAT due whenever it issues an invoice or receives payment, whichever is the earlier – ie it should charge at the higher rate after 1 April, the date of the increase.

reclaiming input VAT

Businesses should claim back the VAT charged by their suppliers in the normal way. Invoices received after the rate change relating to purchases made before the rate change should show VAT at the lower rate: this is the amount that should be reclaimed.

VAT rate changes and special schemes

If a business operates a special VAT scheme, it may be affected by a change in VAT rate. For example:

- a business that uses the **Cash Accounting Scheme** (based on when payments are received) will need to identify sales made before the date the change was made, eg 1 April, and charge VAT on them at the lower rate

- a business that uses the **Flat Rate Scheme** (payments due to HMRC based on a flat percentage – not the VAT rate) will need to use the revised percentage announced by HMRC for use after the change in standard rate

If a business uses the **Annual Accounting Scheme**, there will be no change in the payment of instalments to HMRC.

who needs to know about a VAT rate rise?

A change in the rate of VAT should always be announced by HMRC well in advance of when the change actually comes into force. A business will not only need to notify its own staff, it will also need to notify its customers well in advance.

advising the customers

If the customers of a shop, for example, know about a rise in the VAT rate in advance, they will be motivated to buy more before the rate rise as that way they will obviously pay less.

Therefore, advance notices in shops about a rate rise are very important as this will avoid the inevitable confusion and annoyance of customers when the price paid for goods does increase.

The motor trade does well before a VAT rate rise because a person buying a car may be able to save a large amount of money by paying the lower rate of VAT before the rate rise.

advising the staff

When a VAT rate change is announced by the government all businesses should make plans well in advance to make sure:

- employees know about the change

- the necessary **adjustments are made to computerised accounting software** from the correct date

The areas of a business that will particularly need to know about the changes are:

- accounting and finance staff who deal with **day-to-day transactions involving VAT**, eg invoicing and purchasing

- accounting staff who draw up **financial forecasts**, eg the cash budget – a rise in output VAT charged will increase monthly inflows of cash and will also affect the monthly outflow when the VAT is paid to HMRC

- marketing, sales, and customer services staff create and advise about **price lists**, both online and printed

- shop floor and warehouse staff who deal with **pricing goods**, either with price stickers or bar codes

Most larger businesses are likely to have an action plan on file ready for a VAT rate change and will be able to send out suitable notices and emails in advance. An example of an email (which will be emailed to all management staff) is shown below. The situation here is an increase in standard rate VAT from 20% to 22% on 4 January.

To:	All Departmental Managers
From:	Alex Rowlands, Finance Director
Subject:	Increase in standard rate VAT from 20% to 22% with effect from 4 January

As you will know, standard rate VAT is due to increase from 20% to 22% on 4 January.

It is essential that you all carry out the necessary procedures to ensure that the changeover goes smoothly and that our customers are aware of the price changes. I would like to highlight a number of key areas to you:

1   Accounts Department: Sales and Purchases Ledger should ensure that the updates to the accounting software are downloaded from the software provider's website to amend VAT on invoices and credit notes to 22%.

2   Accounts Department: Management Accounting Section should ensure that the spreadsheets for cash budgets are amended to show the increase in output VAT received.

3   Marketing and Sales: all publicity literature quoting VAT-inclusive prices should be withdrawn before 4 January and revised prices calculated and quoted on new publicity material. The website should be similarly checked for prices and the VAT rate on the online shop amended accordingly from 4 January.

4   Warehouse and shop: any price stickers or barcodes on stock showing pre-increase prices should be removed and replaced by new price stickers and barcodes.

Please ensure that in each case detailed instructions are issued to your staff. These instructions are available as standing instructions in the Company Procedures Manual.

Regards

Alex Rowlands

OTHER AMENDMENTS TO VAT SCHEMES

Although the alteration in the rate of VAT is probably the most common change a business will have to deal with in relation to VAT, there are other areas of change which will need to be communicated to staff by employers. These include:

reporting errors on previous VAT Returns

As we have seen already (on page 80), HMRC allows corrections on VAT Returns for net errors in the calculation of input and output VAT up to a limit of £10,000, or 1% of turnover up to a maximum of £50,000. This may be subject to change in the future. Should this happen, the management of the business would have to communicate the amount of the revised limit to the relevant staff, probably by email, so that the employees responsible for the compilation and authorisation of the VAT Return would comply with the new requirements.

When an error is identified in the current or previous period's VAT Return it is important that the appropriate management of the business are informed of this. They will need to be told whether the error has been corrected in the current return or if it is significant enough that it needs to be disclosed separately. They must also be made fully aware of any penalties or surcharges the business may face if they fail to properly disclose errors or omissions.

change to a special scheme for VAT

As we have already seen in Chapter 3, there are a number of special VAT schemes to help businesses – especially smaller businesses – deal with the administration of VAT in a cost-effective way. These include:

- the **Cash Accounting Scheme**, which is based on accounting for VAT when payments are received and made, rather than when invoices are received and issued

- the **Flat Rate Scheme**, where payments due to HMRC are based on a flat percentage related to the trade in which the business operates

- the **Annual Accounting Scheme** which only requires a VAT Return to be made every twelve months and involves payment of VAT by regular instalments

These schemes are subject to modification from time to time. For example:

- the turnover limit which applies to certain schemes may be raised

- the flat rate percentage which applies to the flat rate scheme for certain types of business may be adjusted when the standard VAT rate changes

In each case the person in charge of VAT administration in the business must communicate the details to the relevant staff. In some cases the business may want to review whether it is worth staying with the special scheme. In other cases, if the annual turnover of the business exceeds the limit applicable to the special scheme, the business may have to withdraw from the scheme. All these factors will need to be communicated within the business and, where necessary, form the basis for internal discussion and possibly also for consultation with the accountants of the business.

ETHICAL BEHAVIOUR IN RELATION TO VAT AND PAYROLL

If you studied the level 2 AAT qualification, you will already have studied professional ethics and will know the importance of accountants complying with the AAT Code of Professional Ethics and adhering to the fundamental ethical principles.

These principles are:

- Integrity
- Objectivity
- Professional competence and due care
- Confidentiality
- Professional behaviour

You need to understand the importance of these ethical principles when dealing with VAT and payroll. The AAT code specifically identifies the importance of acting in good faith and exercising care in relation to facts or information presented on behalf of clients or employers when dealing with HMRC.

All VAT and payroll work must be carried out with integrity and objectivity and must ensure the confidentiality of any personal data that is processed. You must also be aware of the importance of maintaining technical knowledge to ensure all work carried out is with a high degree of professional competence and due care.

When dealing with VAT and payroll matters there may be situations where an accountant faces ethical dilemmas, and their fundamental principles may be threatened.

integrity and objectivity

In certain situations pressure may be put on an accountant to allow irrecoverable VAT (ie VAT on items which the business is not entitled to claim back) to be included on the business's VAT Return. In these situations, the accountant must ensure that they maintain their integrity – the quality of being straightforward and honest – and do not allow that to happen.

An example of this would be if the business purchased a company car for the managing director that they would use for business and private use. We saw in Chapter 3 that VAT on a car cannot usually be claimed back by a business. If the managing director tries to put pressure on the accountant to claim back the VAT on the car, this is not ethical and threatens the accountant's integrity. It is also illegal. In this situation the accountant must stand firm and must not do what the managing director is asking him to.

An accountant must remain objective when dealing with VAT. This means that the accountant must not be influenced by other people's opinions or by their own personal feelings. In the situation above, the managing director could put pressure on the accountant and even threaten them if they do not do as requested. The accountant must ensure that they are not influenced by this pressure and must remain independent, thereby protecting their fundamental principle of objectivity.

An accountant may also face threats to their integrity in relation to payroll. Imagine if a manager asked you to pay some of the production staff 'cash in hand' for some overtime they have done, ie pay them without it going through the payroll system. On the face of it, this would appear to be beneficial for both the business and the workers – the business doesn't have to pay employer's National Insurance or pension contributions on the payments, and the employees don't have to pay tax. However, this is ethically and legally wrong and the accountant should not allow this to happen.

professional competence and due care

It is important that an accountant who is responsible for preparing VAT Returns and payroll submissions is fully aware of the relevant legislation and regulations. Earlier in this chapter we looked at sources of VAT and payroll information and also identified the regulations which apply. In order to comply with the fundamental principle of professional competence and due care, accountants must ensure that they are fully familiar and up-to-date with this information as failure to do so could result in penalties and/or fines for the business.

Members of professional accounting bodies are expected to carry out Continuing Professional Development (CPD) in order to maintain their knowledge and expertise. This may be through attending courses, reading articles or on the job training from more experienced staff. By doing this the accountant will ensure that they continue to act with professional competence. Accountants who are responsible for VAT and/or payroll must ensure that they attain relevant CPD in these areas.

There will be situations where an accountant has a query about VAT or payroll that is beyond their own current experience or expertise. In these situations, they must ensure that the query is referred to a line manager with the appropriate knowledge and expertise and not to deal with it themself.

confidentiality

Accountants must ensure that any information obtained during the course of their professional work is not disclosed to any unauthorised person without proper and specific authority to do so. An accountant who deals with VAT and/or payroll may potentially deal with sensitive and confidential information about the business and its employees, so it is important that they adhere to the fundamental principle of confidentiality, holding this confidential information securely, and only disclosing it when authorised to do so.

We saw in Chapter 5 that employers are required to adhere to strict data protection principles when handling personal information about employees. It is worth recapping these here. Information must be:

■ used fairly, lawfully, and transparently

■ used for specified, explicit purposes

■ used in a way that is adequate, relevant, and limited to only what is necessary

■ accurate and, where necessary, kept up-to-date

■ kept for no longer than is necessary

■ handled in a way that ensures appropriate security, including protection against unlawful or unauthorised processing, access, loss, destruction, or damage

professional behaviour

Accountants must ensure that they do not bring the accounting profession into disrepute by acting in any way that is unprofessional or does not comply with the relevant laws and regulations. Consequently, an accountant who deals with VAT and/or payroll for the business must ensure that the business complies with the VAT legislation detailed earlier in this chapter and with the relevant payroll legislation.

COMMUNICATING WITH HMRC

From time to time, businesses may need to contact HMRC to ask advice about certain VAT and payroll issues. Most queries can be readily answered by the various channels of communication provided to businesses and their advisors by HMRC. The options are:

- via its website

- by email

- by telephone

- by post

online information

The HMRC **website** – www.gov.uk (or simply search for HMRC) – has a powerful search facility and will provide the information to answer many queries which a business may raise, for example:

'Can you give me details of special schemes?'

'What is the definition of a tax point?'

'What goods and services are VAT-exempt?'

'What is the minimum wage?'

emailed enquiries

A business can email enquiries to HMRC, although this can be rather restrictive because HMRC has a number of security processes that need to be cleared before personal information can be transferred by email.

telephone advice

If a business is unable to find the information it needs on the HMRC website, it can **telephone** HMRC, although this can often take longer than emailing, particularly at busy times in the tax or payroll cycles.

writing to HMRC

If a business is having problems finding out the answers to its enquiries online or by telephone, it can resort to the traditional method of communication and write a letter and send it by post. This is becoming an increasingly uncommon method of communication. However, there are still certain situations where written communication is required.

Chapter Summary

■ Accountants must ensure that they report VAT and payroll information to the relevant person in an organisation. This may be the manager or owner of the business, or a client of an accounting practice.

■ Information that is communicated must clearly identify time limits and seek authorisation for submission of VAT Returns and payroll reports, if appropriate.

■ The timing of VAT payments to HMRC can affect the cash flow position of a business. Cash flow can be improved if payment of customer invoices (which include output VAT) is made in advance of the payment of net VAT due to HMRC.

■ VAT law is derived from a number of different sources including:

– UK statute law and statutory instruments

– VAT Notices published by HMRC

■ Changes in VAT and payroll laws and regulations affect businesses in a variety of ways and so it is important that businesses stay up-to-date with:

– VAT rate changes

– changes to the types of goods and services subject to VAT

– changes to special schemes

– changes to regulations affecting wages such as the national minimum wage, personal allowances and National Insurance thresholds

■ Accountants who deal with VAT and payroll must ensure that they adhere to the fundamental ethical principles which are:
– integrity
– objectivity
– professional competence and due care
– confidentiality
– professional behaviour

■ Accountants must be aware of the importance of data protection, information security and confidentiality when dealing with VAT and payroll.

■ Businesses can communicate with HMRC in a variety of ways: online research and enquiries, telephone, email and letter.

Key Terms	**Finance Act**	the UK Act of Parliament passed each year to put into effect changes proposed in the Budget
	Act of Parliament	UK statute passed by both Houses of Parliament which becomes the law enforceable within the UK
	Statutory Instrument	subsidiary rules and regulations which have the force of law and the authority of Parliament
	VAT Notices	regulations imposed by HMRC which have legal force
	AAT Code of Professional Ethics	sets out the fundamental ethical principles that AAT members and student members are expected to adhere to in order to maintain the required standards of professional behaviour
	integrity	accountants should be straightforward and honest in performing professional duties
	objectivity	decisions should be made based on true facts and accountants must not let their own bias or prejudice, or pressure from others, affect decisions that they make
	professional competence and due care	accountants have a duty to ensure that they have the necessary skills to carry out any work that is assigned to them and that they always take sufficient care to ensure that the quality of their work meets the high standards expected of them
	confidentiality	information obtained during the course of professional work should not be disclosed without proper and specific authority or unless there is a legal duty to do so
	Continuing Professional Development	members of professional accounting bodies are expected to keep their technical knowledge up-to-date through relevant study, training and by attending courses
	professional behaviour	accountants should maintain the good reputation of the accounting profession and should not do anything to discredit the accounting profession

Activities

6.1 Roddy works as an assistant accountant at Freshsheen Ltd. He has prepared the draft VAT Return for the business for the quarter ended 31 March, and a summary of the figures is shown here:

	£
Box 1	20,743.20
Box 4	9,441.33
Box 6	103,716
Box 7	67,207

(a) Complete the following information that Roddy should include in an email to his manager before the VAT Return is submitted.

The amount due to HMRC is ……	£
THE VAT Return must be submitted to HMRC by ….	

(b) Roddy has been investigating the possible benefits of moving Freshsheen Ltd to annual accounting for VAT and believes that this would be a good idea for the business. What should he do about his findings?

(a)	Do nothing, he is not senior enough to make this decision	
(b)	Contact HMRC to move the business on to the annual accounting scheme for VAT	
(c)	Discuss his findings with his manager	
(d)	Email the directors of the business directly with a detailed report of his findings	

Which **one** of these options is correct?

6.2 **(a)** You have just completed the monthly wages report for March for the business that you work for based on the schedule of hours worked by each employee that was provided to you by the production manager. The owner of the business is responsible for the day-to-day running of the business but uses an external firm of accountants to prepare the financial statements at the year-end. Who should you send the report to for approval?

(a)	HMRC	
(b)	The production manager	
(c)	The owner of the business	
(d)	The external accountants	

Which **one** of these options is correct?

(b) You have now found out that there has been a change to the national minimum wage from April. The pay rates will need to be amended to reflect this before you run the next wages report. Which of the following sources would you use to find out the correct information about the revised rates?

(a)	Discussion with the production manager	
(b)	Update on the gov.uk website	
(c)	Discussions with other trainee accountants at college	
(d)	Information from the external accountants	

Select **all** options that are correct.

6.3 The cash flow of a business which makes quarterly payments of net VAT to HMRC will improve if:

(a)	The business switches to the VAT annual accounting scheme	
(b)	The business reduces the credit period on its sales invoices from 60 to 30 days of invoice	
(c)	The business pays its suppliers' purchase invoices after 30 days rather than 60 days	

Which **one** of these options is correct?

6.4 Imagine that the government's Budget, and subsequent legislation, states that from 1 January the standard rate of VAT will increase from 20% to 25%.

You run a business that sells adult clothes, all of which are standard-rated for VAT.

Decide whether each of the following statements is true or false.

(a) This increase in VAT will encourage people to buy clothes after 1 January.

True or False?

(b) A customer who receives clothes before 1 January and pays for the goods after 1 January will pay VAT at the lower rate of VAT.

True or False?

6.5 Today's date is 1 September. You work in the Accounts Department of a business and have received an email from your manager telling you that a 5% decrease in the standard rate of VAT will come into effect from 1 October. The current standard rate is 25%.

Complete the gaps in the text of the email using the following words or figures:

| 20% | output | credit notes | 25% | cash budget | decrease |

As you will know, standard rate VAT is due to [   ] from 25% to 20% on 1 October.

It is essential that you all carry out the necessary procedures to ensure that the changeover goes smoothly.

You will need to make sure that:

1   The settings on the computerised accounts system for VAT on standard-rated invoices and [   ] are amended to [   ]

2   All price lists showing VAT at [   ] should be amended to show the lower rate as soon as possible.

3   The [   ] spreadsheets should be amended to show a lower amount of [   ] VAT received on sales invoices.

6.6 You work for a small firm of accountants that prepares VAT Returns for a wide range of clients using an HMRC-approved accounting software package. In which of the following situations would you check whether the accounting software needed to be updated:

(a)	You receive an email from HMRC about a change in VAT legislation	
(b)	Your manager has attended a CPD course where he was told that there may be a change to VAT legislation in six months' time	
(c)	Another trainee accountant at college has told you they have just changed accounting software	
(d)	You receive an email from the software provider suggesting an update is required	

Select **all** options that are correct.

6.7 It is important that accountants who deal with VAT and payroll maintain up-to-date and relevant knowledge about these areas. Adherence to which of the fundamental ethical principles set out in the AAT Code of Professional Ethics will ensure this?

(a)	Integrity	
(b)	Confidentiality	
(c)	Professional behaviour	
(d)	Professional competence and due care	

Which **one** of these options is correct?

Answers to chapter activities

CHAPTER 1: INTRODUCTION TO VALUE ADDED TAX

1.1 (b) Output tax

1.2 (a) A VAT Return

1.3 (b) Output tax minus input tax

1.4 (a) It will decrease the amount due to be paid

1.5 (d) It will increase by £6.70, which is the VAT amount on the credit note

1.6 (d) By the manufacturer and the supplier of the materials for the product and the shop

1.7 (c) The goods are chargeable for VAT, but the rate is 0%

1.8 (b) The value of her taxable supplies over the last twelve months has exceeded the registration threshold set by HMRC

1.9 (a) An individual who sets up a shop in the town where she lives

1.10 (d) His business would benefit because it would be able to reclaim input VAT on standard-rated invoices

1.11 (b) Six years

1.12 (d) Are already VAT-registered, to ensure they are complying with the VAT regulations

1.13 (b) 30 August 2023

1.14 1 February 2023

CHAPTER 2: VAT AND BUSINESS DOCUMENTS

2.1 (c) Invoice number, amount of VAT charged, unit price, VAT rate

2.2 (a) Show the two items on separate lines of the invoice with separate VAT rates and separate VAT amounts

2.3 (d) The amount involved is £250 or less

2.4 two of: no VAT registration number; no VAT rates or amounts listed; not a valid VAT receipt.

2.5 (c) The buyer can send a payment in advance to obtain the goods

2.6 (a) £3.90

2.7 (b) The date the goods are sent to the customer

2.8 (b) The date of the VAT invoice

2.9 (c) Every time an invoice is issued, or a payment is made, whichever is first

2.10 (a) 26 October

2.11 **(a)** 8 April

 (b) £256.50

CHAPTER 3: INPUTS AND OUTPUTS AND SPECIAL SCHEMES

3.1   (b)   Exempt

3.2   (c)   Some goods that are standard-rated and some that are exempt

3.3   (a)   Is charged on costs and expenses that cannot definitely be attributed to standard-rated supplies or to exempt supplies

3.4   (d)   The limit set which enables a partially exempt business to reclaim input VAT paid on exempt supplies

3.5   (d)   You take your employees out for a celebratory meal

3.6   (c)   The business is a car hire firm, and the car will be hired out to customers

3.7   (b)   £405

3.8   (c)   £47.85

3.9   (a)   The VAT Return has to be submitted every 12 months

3.10   (b)   The amount due to HMRC is charged at a fixed rate on the total supplies for each VAT period

3.11   (c)   Allows businesses to account for VAT on the basis of the date of payments received

3.12   (a) is false

(b) & (c) are true

3.13

(a)	This scheme will automatically provide for relief on any bad debt	cash
(b)	A supplier submits a VAT Return once every twelve months	annual
(c)	Payment is charged at a percentage rate related to the type of business	flat
(d)	Payment can be made in nine equal monthly instalments	annual
(e)	This scheme may be operated with the annual accounting scheme	flat <u>or</u> cash
(f)	The VAT Return is due two months after the VAT period	annual
(g)	This scheme accounts for output VAT on the date payment is received	cash
(h)	This scheme does not have to record every single VAT transaction	flat

3.14   (c)   16.5%

Note: because the bookkeeper's expenditure on goods, including VAT, is £1,980, which is less than 2% of their turnover including VAT of £102,240 (£85,200 x 120%), they are classified as a limited cost business and so pay a flat rate of 16.5%.

3.15   (b)   £552.50

CHAPTER 4: THE VAT RETURN, ERRORS, AND PENALTIES

4.1　(b)　Purchases daybook, cash book (payments side), petty cash book (payments)

4.2　(d)　Sales daybook, cash book (receipts side), sales returns daybook

4.3　(c)　Deduct it from the input tax side of the VAT Account as an error correction

4.4　(b)　The accounting software has incorrectly calculated the VAT on the invoice at reduced rate

　　　(d)　Julienne needs to adjust the VAT rate for the supplier in the accounting software

4.5　(c)　Added to the Box 4 figure on the VAT Return

4.6　(a)　Aisha can claim £780

　　　(b)　The earliest point that Aisha can claim bad debt relief on this invoice is the VAT Period ending 31 December

　　　(c)　Aisha will claim the bad debt relief by adding the VAT calculated in (a) to the Box 4 figure on her VAT Return.

4.7　**False**; because Jeanie pays by direct debit the VAT due will be collected a further three days after 7 August, ie 10 August.

4.8　(a)　£540

　　　(b)　This adjustment will decrease input tax on the VAT Return.

4.9　(b)　£10,000

4.10　(c)　Include £170 in Box 1 of the VAT Return

4.11　**(a)**　(a) The accounting software has been incorrectly set up for normal accounting for VAT

　　　(b)

Reconciliation	
	£
VAT liability per the draft VAT Return	5,826.00
Output VAT on closing trade receivables	−7,674.00
Input VAT on closing trade payables	2,347.00
VAT liability per the trial balance	499.00

4.12　(b)　Application programming interface

4.13　**(a)**　(a) Two points

　　　(b)　(c) Four points as Kelpex Ltd submits VAT Returns quarterly

　　　(c)　(a) & (c) are false and (b) is true

4.14 **(a)**   (d) 7 August 2023

      (b)   £660

            Working: Payment was due on 7 August and is 52 days late. So 2% of the amount outstanding on day 15 and 2% of the amount outstanding on day 30.

            First late payment penalty is 4% x £16,500 = £660.

      (c)   £40

            Working: From day 31 to day 53 is 22 days.

            Second late payment penalty is £16,500 x 4% x 22/365 = £39.78 so £40 to the nearest £.

CHAPTER 5: PRINCIPLES OF PAYROLL

5.1   the correct statements are:

      (b)   They must register before the first pay day

      (d)   They must run their payroll using computerised payroll software

      (e)   Individuals who employ staff are required to register as an employer

5.2   (b)   Real Time Information

5.3   HMRC **is** entitled to visit an employer's premises to check its payroll records. If the employer has paid too much it will receive a refund and HMRC will **sometimes** be paid interest on this refund. If the business has not paid enough, it will be asked to pay the additional amount within **30** days. HMRC will **sometimes** charge the employer a penalty if it has unpaid.

5.4

Definition	Payroll term
Tax on deductions from an employee's gross pay on which tax is not due	Tax relief
The amount an employee receives after all deductions	Net pay
An employee's total earnings after any tax-free deductions	Taxable pay
An employee's total earnings before any deductions	Gross pay
A combination of a number and a letter representing how much free pay an employee is entitled to	Tax code

5.5

Deduction	Statutory deduction	Non-statutory deduction
Student loan	✔	
PAYE	✔	
Union subscriptions		✔
Employee's National Insurance Contribution	✔	
Pension	✔	
Donation to charity		✔
Private medical insurance		✔

5.6

Option	May have caused the difference
PAYE	✔
Union subscription	✔
Employee's National Insurance Contribution	✔
Employer's National Insurance Contribution	
Employer's pension contribution	
Employee's pension contribution	✔
Charitable donation	✔
Private medical insurance	✔

5.7　(a)　£100,000

(b)　£5,000

(c)　Employer Payment Summary

5.8

Definition	Payroll term
The form that tells HMRC about expenses and benefits an employee has received in the year	P11D
The form that shows the tax an employee has paid on their earnings in the tax year	P60
The online submission that should be made if the employer has not actually paid anyone in the tax month	EPS
The online submission of pay information to HMRC on, or before, a pay day	FPS
The form that the employer gives to an employee who leaves employment with them. It contains personal and employment data and has a part that needs to be given to the individual's new employer	P45

5.9   (c)   Tax and NIC on 'minor, irregular or impracticable' expenses or benefits given to employees

5.10   (b)   2%

5.11   (b)   £300

5.12

The amount due to HMRC is ……	£2,503.30
This amount must be paid by ….	22 January 2024
The business can pay quarterly as its average monthly PAYE payment is less than ….	£1,500

CHAPTER 6: COMMUNICATING VAT AND PAYROLL INFORMATION

6.1 **(a)**

The amount due to HMRC is ……	£11,301.87
The date the VAT Return must be submitted to HMRC by is ….	7 May

    (b)   (c)   Discuss his findings with his manager

6.2 **(a)**   (c)   The owner of the business

    (b)   (b)   Update on the gov.uk website

          (d)   Information from the external accountants

6.3 (b)   The business reduces the credit period on its sales invoices from 60 to 30 days of invoice

6.4 **(a)**   False

    (b)   True

6.5

> As you will know, standard rate VAT is due to **decrease** from 25% to 20% on 1 October.
>
> It is essential that you all carry out the necessary procedures to ensure that the changeover goes smoothly.
>
> You will need to make sure that:
>
> 1   The settings on the computerised accounts system for VAT on standard-rated invoices and **credit notes** are amended to **20%**.
>
> 2   All price lists showing VAT at **25%** should be amended to show the lower rate as soon as possible.
>
> 3   The **cash budget** spreadsheets should be amended to show a lower amount of **output** VAT received on sales invoices.

6.6 (a)   You receive an email from HMRC about a change in VAT legislation

    (d)   You receive an email from the software provider suggesting an update is required

6.7 (d)   Professional competence and due care

Reference Material

For AAT Assessment of Tax Processes for Business

Finance Act 2023

For assessments from 29 January 2024

Note: This reference material is accessible by candidates during their live computer based assessment for Business Tax.

This material was current at the time this book was published, but may be subject to change. Readers are advised to check the AAT website or Osborne Books website for any updates.

Reference material for AAT assessment of Tax Processes for Businesses

Introduction

This document comprises data that you may need to consult during your Tax Processes for Businesses computer-based assessment.

The material can be consulted during the practice and live assessments by using the reference materials section at each task position. It's made available here so you can familiarise yourself with the content before the assessment.

Do not take a print of this document into the exam room with you*.

This document may be changed to reflect periodical updates in the computer-based assessment, so please check you have the most recent version while studying. This version is based on Finance Act 2023 and is for use in AAT Q2022 assessments in 2024.

*Unless you need a printed version as part of reasonable adjustments for particular needs, in which case you must discuss this with your tutor at least six weeks before the assessment date.

Note that page numbers refer to those in the original AAT Guidance document

Contents

1. Rates of VAT

Taxable supplies:

Standard rate	20%
Reduced rate	5%
Zero rate	0%

Non-taxable supplies have no VAT applied:

- Exempt
- Outside the scope of VAT

2. Registration and deregistration for VAT

Registration threshold	£85,000
Deregistration threshold	£83,000

Compulsory registration	Notify HMRC	Registration effective from
Historic test	Within 30 days of the end of the month threshold was exceeded	First day of the second month after threshold exceeded
Future test	Before the end of the 30 day period	From the start of the 30 day period

Deregistration	Notify HMRC	Deregistration effective from
Compulsory	Within 30 days of the business ceasing to make taxable supplies	Date of cessation
Voluntary	Evidence that taxable supplies will not exceed the VAT deregistration threshold in the next 12 months	Date request received by HMRC, or Agreed later date

3. Failure to register for VAT

- This can result in a penalty for failure to notify. The penalty is a % of potential lost revenue (PLR).

Type of behaviour	Within 12 months of tax being due		12 months or more after tax was due	
	unprompted	prompted	unprompted	prompted
Non-deliberate	0-30%	10-30%	10-30%	20-30%
Deliberate	20-70%	35-70%	20-70%	35-70%
Deliberate and concealed	30-100%	50-100%	30-100%	50-100%

- Penalties will not be applied if there is a reasonable excuse.

- HMRC will treat the business as though it had registered on time and will expect VAT to be accounted for as if it had been charged. The business has two choices:

    i. treat the invoices as VAT inclusive and absorb the VAT which should have been charged, or

    ii. account for VAT as an addition to the charges already invoiced and attempt to recover this VAT from its customers.

4. Changes to the VAT registration

HMRC must be notified of a change of:

Name, trading name or address	Within 30 days
Partnership members	Within 30 days
Agent's details	Within 30 days
Bank account details	14 days in advance
Change in business activity	Within 30 days

5. Keeping business and VAT records

Record retention period	6 years
Penalty for failure to keep records	£500

6. Contents of a VAT invoice

Full VAT invoice

- a sequential number based on one or more series which uniquely identifies the document
- the time of the supply (tax point)
- the date of issue of the document (where different to the time of supply)
- supplier's name, address, and VAT registration number
- customer's name and address
- a description sufficient to identify the goods or services supplied
- for each description, the quantity of the goods or the extent of the services, the rate of VAT, and the amount payable excluding VAT — this can be expressed in any currency
- the gross total amount payable, excluding VAT — this can be expressed in any currency
- the rate of any cash discount offered
- the total amount of VAT chargeable — this must be expressed in sterling
- the unit price (applicable to countable elements).

Simplified VAT invoices (<£250)

- suppliers name, address, and VAT registration number
- the time of supply (tax point)
- a description which identifies the goods or services supplied
- for each applicable VAT rate, the total amount payable, including VAT, and the VAT rate.

Modified VAT invoices

- a full VAT invoice showing the VAT inclusive rather than VAT exclusive values.

7. Partial exemption for VAT

De minimis amount	£625 per month
Proportion of total input VAT	<50%

- Generally, a partially exempt business cannot reclaim the input tax paid on purchases that relate to exempt supplies.

- If the amount of input tax incurred relating to exempt supplies is below a minimum de minimis amount, input tax can be reclaimed in full.

- If the amount of input tax incurred relating to exempt supplies is above the de minimis amount, only the part of the input tax that related to non-exempt supplies can be reclaimed.

8.   International trade and VAT

Export of goods	Zero-rated
Import of goods	UK VAT applied using postponed accounting.
Export of services	Apply UK VAT if place of supply is in the UK: • for supplies to business, place of supply is the location of the customer (outside the scope of UK VAT) • for supplies to non-business customers, place of supply is the location of the supplier (charge UK VAT).
Import of services	Reverse charge applies

9.   Tax points for VAT

Basic tax point date	Date of despatch of the goods/carrying out of the service
Actual tax point date may be earlier	If either: • payment is received earlier • invoice is issued earlier. Actual tax point becomes the earlier of these two dates.
Actual tax point date may be later	If: • invoice is issued within 14 days of despatch/service (and advance payment didn't apply).

- Deposits are treated separately to final payment and so may have a different tax point.
- The tax point is always the date of payment if cash basis is being applied.
- Where services are being supplied on a continuous basis over a period in excess of a month but invoices are being issued regularly throughout the period, a tax point is created every time an invoice is issued or a payment is made, whichever happens first.
- Goods on sale or return will have a tax point date either on adoption (the customer indicates they will keep the goods) or 12 months after removal of the goods where this is earlier.

10.   Time limits for issuing a VAT invoice

Within 30 days of tax point which is either:

- within 30 days of date of supply or
- within 30 days of payment if payment was in advance.

11.   Blocked expenses and VAT

Input VAT cannot be recovered on blocked expenses.

Business entertainment

- The exception is that input tax can be reclaimed in respect of entertaining overseas customers, but not UK or Isle of Man customers.

- When the entertainment is in respect of a mixed group of both employees and non-employees (e.g. customers and/or suppliers), the business can only reclaim VAT on the proportion of the expenses that is for employees and on the proportion for overseas customers.

Cars

- Input VAT can only be recovered on cars if it is wholly for business (no private use).

- 50% of input VAT can be recovered when cars are hired/leased.

- VAT can be recovered on commercial vehicles such as vans/lorries.

Assets with private use

- The VAT recovery should be based only on the proportion related to business use.

12.   Fuel scale charge and VAT

If the business pays for road fuel, it can deal with the VAT charged on the fuel in one of four ways:

- reclaim all of the VAT. All of the fuel must be used only for business purposes

- reclaim all of the VAT and pay the appropriate fuel scale charge (as follows) - this is a way of accounting for output tax on fuel that the business buys but that is then used for private motoring

- reclaim only the VAT that relates to fuel used for business mileage. Detailed records of business and private mileage must be kept

- do not reclaim any VAT. This can be a useful option if mileage is low and also if fuel is used for both business and private motoring. If the business chooses this option it must apply it to all vehicles, including commercial vehicles.

The fuel scale charge is as follows:

Description of vehicle: vehicle's CO2 emissions figure	VAT inclusive consideration for a 12 month prescribed accounting period (£)	VAT inclusive consideration for a 3 month prescribed accounting period (£)	VAT inclusive consideration for a 1 month prescribed accounting period (£)
120 or less	737	183	61
125	1,103	276	91
130	1,179	293	97
135	1,250	312	103
140	1,327	331	110
145	1,398	349	115
150	1,474	368	122
155	1,545	386	128
160	1,622	405	134
165	1,693	423	140
170	1,769	441	146
175	1,840	459	152
180	1,917	478	159
185	1,988	497	164
190	2,064	515	171
195	2,135	534	178
200	2,212	552	183

Description of vehicle: vehicle's CO_2 emissions figure	VAT inclusive consideration for a 12 month prescribed accounting period (£)	VAT inclusive consideration for a 3 month prescribed accounting period (£)	VAT inclusive consideration for a 1 month prescribed accounting period (£)
205	2,283	571	190
210	2,359	588	195
215	2,430	607	202
220	2,507	626	208
225 or more	2,578	644	214

- Where the CO_2 emission figure is not a multiple of 5, the figure is rounded down to the next multiple of 5 to determine the level of the charge.

13. Bad debt and VAT

VAT that has been paid to HMRC and which has not been received from the customer can be reclaimed as bad debt relief. The conditions are that:

  i.   the debt is more than six months and less than four years and six months old

  ii.   the debt has been written off in the VAT account and transferred to a separate bad debt account

  iii. the debt has not been sold or handed to a factoring company

  iv.   the business did not charge more than the normal selling price for the items.

Bad debt relief does not apply when the cash accounting scheme is used because the VAT is not paid to HMRC until after the customer has paid it to the supplier.

14. Due dates for submitting the VAT return and paying electronically

Deadline for submitting return and paying VAT – quarterly accounting	1 month and 7 days after the end of the VAT period
Deadline if being paid by direct debit	HMRC will collect 3 working days after the submission deadline.

- Please see alternative submission and payment deadlines for special accounting schemes.

15. Special accounting schemes for VAT

15.1 Annual accounting scheme for VAT

Joining the scheme	Maximum (estimated) taxable turnover in next 12 months	£1.35m
Leaving the scheme	Compulsory if taxable turnover at the end of the VAT accounting year exceeds the threshold	£1.6m
VAT returns	One annual return	2 months after the end of the accounting period
VAT payments (monthly)	Nine monthly interim payments (10% of estimated VAT bill based on previous returns)	At the end of months 4 to 12 in the accounting period
	Balancing payment	2 months after the end of the accounting period
VAT payments (quarterly)	Three interim payments (25% of estimated VAT bill based on previous returns)	At the end of months 4, 7 and 10 in the accounting period
	Balancing payment	2 months after the end of the accounting period

15.2 Cash accounting scheme for VAT

Joining the scheme	Maximum (estimated) taxable turnover in next 12 months	£1.35m
Leaving the scheme	Compulsory if taxable turnover at the end of the VAT accounting year exceeds the threshold	£1.6m

15.3 Flat Rate Scheme for VAT

Joining the scheme	Taxable turnover (excluding VAT) in the next 12 months	£150,000
Leaving the scheme	On the anniversary of joining, turnover in the last 12 months (including VAT) or expected turnover in next 12 months	£230,000
Discount	In first year of being VAT-registered	1%
Limited cost business	Goods cost less than either: • 2% of turnover, or • £1,000 a year	16.5%
Capital expenditure	Input tax can be recovered on individual large capital purchases	£2,000

- The appropriate flat rate % will be provided in the assessment.

16. Errors in previous VAT returns

Adjustments can be made to correct errors that are:

- below the reporting threshold
- not deliberate
- for an accounting period that ended less than 4 years ago.

The reporting threshold is;

- £10,000 or less or
- up to 1% (maximum £50,000) of total value of sales and all other outputs excluding any VAT
- When the next VAT return is submitted, the net value is added to VAT due on sales and other outputs for tax due to HMRC, or to VAT reclaimed in the period on purchases and other inputs for tax due to you.

If the value of the net VAT error discovered is above the reporting threshold, it must be declared to HMRC separately, in writing.

17. Late submission and late payment of VAT

17.1 Late submission

Submission frequency	Penalty point threshold	Period of compliance
Annual	2 points	24 months
Quarterly	4 points	12 months

Initial penalty	£200
Subsequent penalty	£200

Removal of penalty points

Business has not reached penalty threshold	Each point automatically expires two years from the first day of the month after the month when the late submission occurred.
Business has reached penalty threshold	All points will be reset to zero if both conditions below are met: • a period of compliance (meeting all submission obligations on time for the period of compliance), and • all submissions due in the preceding 24 months have been made (whether or not they were on time).

17.2 Late payment

Number of days overdue	First late payment penalty	Second late payment penalty
up to 15	None	None
16 to 30	2% on the VAT outstanding at day 15 *	None
31 or more	2% on the VAT outstanding at day 15 AND 2% on the VAT outstanding at day 30	A daily rate based on 4% per annum charged every day from day 31 until paid in full

* HMRC have stated that the first late payment penalty which applies to the first 30 days will not be charged until after 31 December 2023.

17.3   Interest charged

Interest is calculated at the Bank of England base rate plus 2.5%.

The Bank of England base rate will be given in the assessment.

18.   Assessment of VAT

If a VAT Return is not submitted on time, HMRC will issue a 'VAT notice of assessment of tax' which will state how much HMRC think is owed.

If HMRC issue an assessment that is too low, a penalty of up to 30% can be charged for not telling them it is incorrect within 30 days.

19. Penalties for inaccuracies in VAT return

A penalty can be charged as a percentage of the potential lost revenue (PLR):

Type of behaviour	Unprompted disclosure %	Prompted disclosure %
Careless	0-30	15-30
Deliberate	20-70	35-70
Deliberate and concealed	30-100	50-100

20. Payroll record retention

Retention period	3 years
Penalty for failure to maintain records	£3,000

21. Types of payroll submission

Full payment submission (FPS)

- File on or before employees pay day.
- Include payments to and deductions for all employees.

Employer payment summary (EPS)

- File if no employees were paid in the month.
- Send by the 19th of the following tax month.

22. Payroll deadlines

Registering for PAYE	You must register before the first payday. You cannot register more than 2 months before you start paying people
Month end date for PAYE	5th of each month
Payment date for monthly payroll	22nd of each month if paid electronically. 19th otherwise. If monthly amounts are <£1,500, quarterly payments can be made
Provide employees with P60	31st May
Filing deadline for Expenses & Benefits forms	6th July
PAYE and Class 1A NIC payment date	22nd July if paying electronically. 19th July otherwise
PAYE settlement agreement submission date	31st July
PAYE and Class 1B NIC payment date	22nd October if paying electronically. 19th October otherwise

23. Penalties for late submission of payroll filings

Penalties may apply if:
- the FPS was late
- the expected amount of FPSs was not filed
- an EPS was not filed.

Number of employees	Monthly penalty
1 to 9	£100
10 to 49	£200
50 to 249	£300
250 or more	£400

Penalties may not apply if:

- the FPS is late but all reported payments on the FPS are within three days of the employees' payday (unless there is regular lateness)
- a new employer is late but sends the first FPS within 30 days of paying an employee
- it is a business's first failure in the tax year to send a report on time.

24. Penalties for late payroll payment

Late payment of monthly/quarterly payments

- The first failure to pay in a tax year does not count as a default.
- Late payment penalties apply to late payments and payments of less than is due.

Number of defaults in a tax year	Penalty percentage applied to the amount that is late in the relevant tax month
1 to 3	1%
4 to 6	2%
7 to 9	3%
10 or more	4%

Additional penalties will apply if:

A monthly or quarterly amount remains outstanding after 6 months	5% of unpaid tax
A monthly or quarterly amount remains outstanding after 12 months	A further 5% of unpaid tax

These additional penalties apply even where only one payment in the tax year is late.

Late payments of amounts due annually or occasionally

30 days late	5%
6 months late	Additional 5%
12 months late	Additional 5%

25. Penalties for inaccuracies in payroll filings

A penalty can be charged as a percentage of the potential lost revenue (PLR):

Type of behaviour	Unprompted disclosure %	Prompted disclosure %
Careless	0-30	15-30
Deliberate	20-70	35-70
Deliberate and concealed	30-100	50-100

Index

for your notes

for your notes

for your notes

for your notes

for your notes

for your notes

for your notes

for your notes

for your notes

for your notes

for your notes

for your notes

for your notes

for your notes

for your notes

for your notes

for your notes